"Tony Harris is a "voice in the wilderness" of the world of marketing revealing important things hidden from the vast majority of us... An important read for any one who wants to live wisely in a rapidly evolving consumer culture."

"Whoa. Buy it for the title, stay for Harris' x-ray vision and synthesis of what's next. Middle path thinking and a look under the covers of how marketers manipulate - and what easy marks we are!"

"In-your-face insights about how marketers get us and keep us coming back for more. Lifts the veil on how we're sold. Read it and be more aware... and wary!"

"A "must read" for CEO's, marketing professionals, consumers. I've been a marketing professional for decades and this book was an eye opener and a game changer for me!"

FADS
MARKETING™

FOOD, ALCOHOL, DRUGS, SEX,
AND THE NEW MARKETING WORLD ORDER

TONY HARRIS

THINC B2B
7419 Olivetas Avenue
La Jolla, CA 92037
www.thincb2b.com

Copyright 2018 by Tony Harris
Published in 2018 by Tony Harris
Cover and book design by Carissa Andrews
Edited by Kate-Madonna Hindes
All rights reserved.
First Edition

ISBN-13:
978-0-692-04171-0 (paperback)
978-1-7329070-0-3 (ebook)
978-1-7329070-1-0 (audio)

Follow FADS Marketing™ on Social Media
facebook.com/thefadsbook
twitter.com/thefadsbook
instagram.com/thefadsbook

This book is dedicated to my family. To my wife Joy, and twin sons Tyler and Mitchell: thank you for your unconditional love, support, and patience.

This book is also dedicated to my dear friends Kim Opitz (kimopitz.com) and Sally McGraw (sallymcgraw.com).
Thank you for bringing my vision to life.

TABLE OF CONTENTS

INTRODUCTION

THIS BOOK ISN'T WHAT YOU THINK IT IS.

This isn't another book about advertising. Advertising as you know it is dead. For businesses that have yet to embrace reality, it's buried and gone. These businesses are the same kind that promote their products or services like a garage sale, telling you to "pop over" and visit. This isn't about the pizza places and accounting groups who send people outside to dance on street corners and wiggle their signs, clamoring for your attention as you drive past, too busy to stop.

This book is about something much simpler and yet, annoyingly complex. How have marketers gotten so damn good at figuring out what you want and finding the scientific formula to make you want it more? You know... to want it *BAD*.

Businesses that are committed to success in the global digital economy are focused on something different: behavior modification. The people behind the scenes—such as myself—we're not interested in changing your mind, and we don't waste time or money to capture you in a random moment. We're laser-focused on changing the very essence of who you are by modifying your behavior. Permanently.

Welcome to the new world. We're designing it for you, around you, and most of all—in your head. We count on the fact that either you don't know, or you are indifferent. And if you're like most people, it's both.

In short, thanks for your data.

You need no introduction, and neither do I...

I was working out in a hotel gym, watching television with the sound turned off. Something struck me about the commercials. There it was, on repeat: Food. Alcohol. Drugs. Sex. (or in short, FADS.) With all the layers of noise and messaging peeled away, I started to see the subtlety of the ads and what they were trying to accomplish. There it was, right in front of my face: the manipulation and incessant drive toward behavior modification.

For the next three hours, I finished my workout and watched in silence. Right before my eyes were brands in overdrive, making their advertisements all about FADS.

I knew I had to figure out a way to talk about FADS, and how they're a significant part of the manipulation that enables behavior modification. FADS influence your behavior and decisions related to food, alcohol, drugs, sex. They have since the beginning of time, as you'll see. But with technology, data tracking, and artificial intelligence crawling into all the nooks and crannies of our lives, those same FADS have become a vehicle for changing your mind, in ways you've never thought before.

Until now.

The truth is, I already know a lot about you. For 25 years, I've worked with brands in lifestyle, sports, entertainment, and technology. I've counseled executives, corporations, and teams marketing to consumers all around the globe. From Japan to Munich, Australia to Taiwan, and the United States to China, I've already worked my way into your head—you just don't know it yet.

I eat, sleep, and breathe the kind of information that helps my clients decide how to market, remarket, retarget, and influence your very thoughts, decisions, and actions.

I've studied data from your buying profile.

I've consulted on the behavioral modeling systems that shape your world.

I've pioneered customer segmentation techniques and popped you into just the right category.

I've visited the place where your phone was made. I talked to the people who sold the parts that went into your phone. And, I've stood on the factory floor where your phone was created.

I also know which credit card you use, when you use it, where you use it, and what you purchase on it. And I know how to use that detailed data to inform and change the content that is specifically curated for you and delivered to your social feeds, your email, your browser experience.

These companies aren't pursuing you. They've already got you.

For a long time, brands focused on answering the question, "How do we get people to buy our product?" After all, marketing and advertising were designed solely to elicit a response; that's not good enough anymore. My clients want more—they want a deeper connection to why you make the decisions you do.

It's why I work with brands to change your behavior, which means changing your tastes. Your pleasure thoughts. The core of your beliefs and how you were raised. I determine the most effective strategies of behavior modification through data and marketing, essentially, changing your entire decision-tree structure. You gave me the data with your "likes" and access to apps. You paved the road with the best intentions of connecting with other people—just like you. I just drove a Maserati down your yellow-brick highway to give everyone else what they wanted all along: your data.

Here's an example: Take your phone. Phones have become so ubiquitous, so woven into your everyday nature that you can't live without them. Your behavior has been modified to the point that you swipe your phone thousands of times a day and never think about it. If the phone isn't charged or anywhere near you, you feel like you're missing an appendage, missing something from your life that's a critical need. Technology has enabled a change in behavior modification. I'm not interested in simply changing your perception of a product. I just want you to live in such a way that without it, you're lost. Ever wonder how the perfect content, clothing, experience, makeup, and messaging finds you?

That's the Powers that Be (PtB) at work—and they're part of this story. They're the collective brains and master planners using business data intelligence to deploy the marketing strategies and ad campaigns you can't ignore. They also bank on the fact that attention spans diminish by the day. Your panties might be in a bunch over privacy issues today, but something shiny will distract you again tomorrow.

MAKING YOU WANT IT, *BAD.*

Here's why you want it all: *You've been made to want it—it's as simple as that.*

Let's look at great milk imposters; first, it was soy, then almond, and soon it'll be another NEW type of protein-rich milk to grab your attention. I know what you're thinking, you FEEL better when you drink different milk, right? Of course, you do—that's the placebo effect in action. Science has proven it... most of the benefit you feel when you consume your overpriced non-lactose milk is mind over matter. That's because the professionals in my line of work know how to manipulate you. It's a tough word for many people to believe, but let me say it again: we manipulate you to choose certain products, eat certain foods, think certain ways, and believe certain things. Soon, everything that now makes up your life will become cultural. Your choices were never really free will, but you being manipulated and plied into thinking what you were doing was personalizing your life with everything from what you drink to what you wear and how you speak.

Do I have your attention yet?

50 - 60 years ago, advertisements were all words. Now it's entirely the opposite. Ad agencies are paid six figures (or more) to take one Instagram image, add a catchphrase and disperse it to the public. So, knowing that we're desensitized by the images and sounds we hear on a daily basis, brands have reworked how to capture our attention —stimulating our senses more and more. You see, that's how FADS become relevant in a technology-enabled environment. *They burn so hot* because messaging is so frequent, focused, and targeted that it's almost like an echo. *A brand echo.* Because you eat it up, the beast is fed more and more.

Stores make decisions based on organic and paid search, so they know when you search and what you search for—that's how they decide how to stock the shelves and how often products should be replenished. Don't assume Home Depot doesn't know whether you're going to buy that wainscot paneling in the store or online. They can count the minutes and hours it took you to act, the credit card you used, and what else you purchased. The PtB know you bought a certain brand, and they might start hitting you up for a related product with even better margins. You see it as helpful, and they see you as a pawn.

You won't like hearing this, but you're easily manipulated. ALL humans are easily manipulated. It might take one or two tries, but eventually, I'm going to capture you very neatly in data sets and subsets that bring my clients dollar bills. Eventually, your behavior will modify. You won't even realize it's happening.

And that's where FADS come in. FADS rise quickly, burn hot, and fall out. They say a lot about who we are and what we're becoming. FADS say you're fat, you're no fun, you need to relax, and you might even die alone. We're counting on the fact you already believe all of that.

1

FOOD

TAKE A SEAT AT THE TABLE; WE'RE JUST GETTING STARTED

*Exploring the link between food advertising trends
and what you're really hungry for*

There must've been a time when humans followed our lizard brain instincts about food.

10,000 years ago, when we were hunter-gatherers, no one suggested we count calories or monitor carb intake; we ate what we could catch as often as we could catch it. Food was fuel, plain and simple. Certainly not the freakish obsession it is today. (We're looking at you, pea protein.)

Sadly, the age of un-influenced appetite is thousands of years in our collective past. As far back as 800 B.C.E., the ancient Greeks had already begun to fret over appetite and intake. They believed that maintaining a balanced, sensible diet was a "civic responsibility," and openly scorned overindulgence.[1] Fast-forward to the fourth century C.E. and holy hermit Evagrius Ponticus slapped the Christian stamp of disapproval on overeating by making "gluttony" one of the Seven Deadly Sins.[2] Skip to the 1840s, and you'll find Presbyterian minister Sylvester Graham insisting that a plain, virtually flavor-free diet was essential for women who wanted to remain both healthy and morally stable. "Spices, stimulants, and other overindulgences lead to indigestion, illness, sexual excess, and civil disorder," Graham insisted.[3] Despite a lack of evidence that linked rosemary to rioting, women all over the American East Coast bought into his misguided philosophy.

Thus, the link between judging people's eating habits and controlling their eating behaviors was born. (A link we'll explore fully in the upcoming pages.) Of course, our collective preoccupation with food and eating is also anchored in our desire to look good. As soon as we understood that food intake impacted physical appearance, we began monitoring every morsel and mouthful—like the gluttonous heathens we are. Not a minute later, marketers took notice.

How we think about food has become a deeply-polarized process. At one end of the spectrum, we have paleo dieters who refuse to eat anything processed, dairy-based, or otherwise absent from a caveman's menu. At the other end, we have molecular gastronomists studying the chemical processes that occur during cooking and tempting us with fake caviar made from "spherified" apples and a multitude of flavored foams.[4] As consumers, we're bombarded by advertising campaigns spewing messages about healthy eating, indulgent eating, simple eating, complex eating, trendy eating, ancient eating... and, well, good luck remembering why you walked into the kitchen in the first place.

What Marketers Know: Food-related Trigger Points

Tactically speaking, food marketers have begun to use a mix of standby methods and intriguing new approaches to influence consumer behaviors. Let's start by examining how modern food, restaurant, diet, and grocery store campaigns are taking a new approach to make you want it bad.

Emotions, Eating, and Emotional Eating

Since food and eating have become highly emotional for many consumers, food marketers frequently focus on feelings. This is a tried-and-true psychological tactic. Multiple studies have shown that emotionally charged messages have a deeper impact on consumers than descriptions of features and functions. This means that many advertising copywriters choose to muse on how a product—coconut water or almond butter, for instance—will make consumers *feel* and how it will improve their lives.[5] In 2012, the *Journal of Advertising Research* published a paper by Orlando Wood of London's Brainjuicer Labs, who presented his findings on how conventional pre-testing measures of persuasion, cut-through, and message receipt have become outdated, and new emotion-based criteria for understanding efficacy need to be implemented.[6]

Data also show us that emotional campaigns are about twice as likely to generate substantial profit gains than rational appeals,[7] so the motivation to pull on consumer heartstrings is strong.

This manifests in food marketing in a staggeringly diverse spread of campaigns. Let's look at two that approach consumer emotions from very different standpoints and with unrelated aims.

CAMPAIGN OF NOTE: #WeighThis, 2015

Accompanied by the inevitable hashtag, frozen diet meal purveyor Lean Cuisine's "#WeighThis" campaign takes a page from the body-positive playbook. The campaign begins as a diverse group of women approach a scale. Instead of stepping on it, an off-camera voice asks them, "What do you feel has been your biggest accomplishment?" Stories of world travel, making the dean's list, donating bone marrow, single motherhood, and weight lifting follow. Then the words, "If you're going to weigh something, weigh what matters" slide across the screen, and we see those same women placing textbooks, barbells, and backpacks on the scale, talking about how their achievements mean so much more than their weight. Meanwhile, on the other side of the screen, viewers surreptitiously wipe away sympathetic tears.

Although this ad is indirect and doesn't urge viewers to run out and stock up on Lean Cuisine meals, its branding impact was decidedly positive. In a May 2014 article, *Forbes* reported, "In testing, this ad proved to be driven by relevance, a clear indicator that the message is something most people can relate to. Brand perception change was a clear driver for success as well, with a score 11 percent above the category norm."[8] By positioning itself as a company that cares and reminding viewers that weight doesn't define us, Lean Cuisine broadcasts compassion, acceptance, and camaraderie. They're saying, "We know losing weight is hard, and also that you'll still be amazing even if you don't lose those last five pounds. We're your supportive partner in this journey."

They're also skating on thin ice by addressing their target market of dieters, and telling them that losing weight is inconsequential. And yet, as the body image crisis builds and social views of dieting shift, Lean Cuisine is not alone in feeling the need to toe that line.

CAMPAIGN OF NOTE: Save the Food, 2016

"The Extraordinary Life and Times of Strawberry" aired as part of a pro-bono campaign created by SapientNitro* for The Ad Council. (*Now known as SapientRazorfish, after a November 2016 merger. As it relates to discussing this campaign, I'll reference the original name of the company that created the work.)

Its goal? To highlight the issue of consumer food waste.

Nearly 40 percent of all food purchased in the U.S. each year gets thrown away uneaten, chalking up a staggering bill of $162 billion,[9] and the Natural Resources Defense Council commissioned this campaign to raise awareness.

In the ad, consumers follow a single strawberry from its early days on the vine, through harvest, transit, packaging, purchase, and moldering away in someone's refrigerator drawer. Accompanied by wistful music taken from the Pixar film "Up," and the occasional amusing Barry White interlude, the spot is filmed from the berry's point of view, casting it as an appealing protagonist—complete with an unrequited crush on a lime! In two minutes, our hero goes from hopeful, young strawberry to inedible garbage. The ad informs us "Wasting food wastes everything: Water, Labor, Fuel, Money, Love." The viewer is left feeling hope, amusement, disappointment, and finally guilt.[10]

"The Extraordinary Life and Times of Strawberry" was just one arm of "Save the Food." Print, web, and out-of-home ads were also created and deployed, urging people to "Cook it. Store it. Share it." rather than trashing perfectly good perishables. AdWeek's coverage of this campaign focuses on how it connects saving food to saving money. Gary Koepke, North American chief creative officer at SapientNitro, is quoted as saying, "We know that moms are compelled by facts that tie food waste to household finances, so the campaign emphasizes this information."[11] That final pang of guilt seems like an equally potent emotional motivator; the underlying message is, "When you waste food, YOU'RE DESTROYING THE PLANET, YOU GOON!" And it undoubtedly resonates with increasingly environmentally conscious consumers, many of whom are composting and urban-gardening out of guilt in the first place.

Food and feelings go hand-in-hand in countless other successful marketing campaigns. Consider how McDonald's early advertisements introduced the public to both speed and low-cost food offerings in the 1950s and 1960s. As consumer mindsets shifted a decade later, so did the messaging, ("You Deserve a Break Today.") In the current age of advertising, McDonald's has chosen to focus on fun, family, and happiness with the "I'm Lovin' It" campaign.[12] The chain-restaurant titan isn't selling burgers and fries; it's selling enjoyment, ease, and relaxation.

Coca-Cola has gone down a similar path, launching "Open Happiness" in 2009, and "Taste the Feeling" in 2016.[13] Apparently, feelings taste like carbonation and corn syrup. *Who knew?*

Emotions and sensations are close cousins, so now let's dive into food marketing that plays on sensory experiences and longings.

The Five Senses and Stuffing our Faces

Campaigns that appeal to our base senses are nothing new, but the body of research supporting their efficacy continues to grow. Aradhna Krishna, director of the Sensory Marketing Laboratory at the University of Michigan, is considered a top expert in the field and is building a storehouse of data linking sensory perceptions with emotional associations. In her 2013 book, *Customer Sense: How the 5 Senses Influence Buying Behavior*, she posits that human senses amplify each other when they are somehow congruent. For instance, Krishna observed that people believed the scent of cinnamon made a heating pad more effective and concluded that since cinnamon suggests warmth, it pairs naturally with actual, physical heat.

When it comes to sensory marketing, *Harvard Business Review* points out, "Such influences are subtle—and that's exactly why they are so powerful. Consumers don't perceive them as marketing messages and therefore don't react with the usual resistance to ads and other promotions."[14]

An unexpected purveyor of subtle sensory manipulation? *Cheese-mongers.*

You likely knew that absolutely no cheese created by earthlings is naturally orange in color. What you might *not* know is that experts believe cheesemakers have been adding artificial color to their delicious dairy products for nearly 500 years.[15] There are three conflicting theories on their motivations:

Cheese-coloring theory 1: Sometime in the 16th century, English farmers realized they could skim fat from the milk they used to make cheese and transform it into butter. However, low-fat cheese was both paler in color and less rich-tasting. When consumers made this mental connection and started passing up sallow-looking cheeses, farmers compensated by adding artificial coloring, making it hard to tell a full-fat cheese from a skimmed one.[16]

Cheese-coloring theory 2: Back then, cheese made in spring and summer was naturally more yellowish since the cows were eating fresh grass instead of dried grains. (Grass has lots of beta-carotene, a naturally occurring orange pigment that ends up in the milk, then the cheese.) Farmers might not have been skimming fat, but began adding colorant, so their cheeses looked identical year-round.[17]

Cheese-coloring theory 3: Since all cheese was white, adding color made certain varieties stand out. In the 17th century, British farmers started adding a vegetable dye called annatto to Red Leicester cheese, so it looked distinct from its cheesy competition.[18]

Whatever the reason, the choices these farmers made five centuries ago still influence consumers today. Although some have gotten used to white cheddars, many others insist on orange cheese; pale cheese just doesn't taste as good.

This notion is supported by the evolution of margarine starting in the late 1800s. This butter substitute is naturally white, but consumers were so used to seeing *yellow* butter that spreading *white* goo on their morning toast felt deeply wrong. For margarine to convince people it *tasted* like butter, it needed to *look* more like butter[19] ... and thus, we have the shockingly-yellow-butter-wannabes of the 21st century. The dyes used are completely tasteless, yet essential to the sensory experience. As science journalist Sara Chodosh points out, "Our perception of a food affects how we think it tastes, and thus orange cheeses and yellow butters seem different than pale products."[20] The visual is linked to the gustatory, thanks to years of farmer-driven subversive marketing.

To this day, food manufacturers and ad agencies continue to cross-pollinate our various senses to make us want, buy, and scarf down their products.

CAMPAIGN OF NOTE: McCain Foods, 2012

This Canadian company is the world's largest manufacturer of frozen potato products[21] and has recently started tinkering with some innovative ways to entice grocery shoppers to buy more spuds on ice.

In 2012, McCain partnered with ad agency Beattie McGuinness Bungay on a £1.4 million campaign for frozen baked potatoes. Ten bus shelters across the United Kingdom were decked out with giant print ads and oversized fiberglass potatoes. When pressed, the fake-potatoes both heated up and emitted the scent of real potatoes, and the potato-fondler was rewarded with a printed coupon to purchase McCain Ready Made Jackets.[22] (Jacket potato = baked potato, for you non-Brits.) The location of these ads was strategic; people at bus stops are often on their way home from work, thinking about dinner, and highly susceptible to suggestion. (And, as we've all been told 6 trillion times, smell is our most emotional sense,[23] so perhaps this campaign was designed to tinker with both emotions *and* senses.)

McCain's marketing director at time of writing, Mark Hodge, has said he plans for more campaigns that play on the senses. "You need to think about how your brand can surprise and connect with people," he told *Marketing Week*. "You must know when the consumer will be most receptive, so you have their attention."[24]

In the same year, Dunkin' Donuts launched a similar effort in Seoul: The company installed atomizers on municipal buses, and whenever the company's jingle was played over the PA, the scent of coffee filled the air. Dunkin' Donuts reported a 16 percent spike in visitors at shops near bus stops frequented by busses fitted with atomizers, and a 29 percent spike in overall coffee sales during the run of the campaign.[25]

So far, we've focused on how marketers manipulate our appetites, but many campaigns are designed to impact our food buying and prepping behaviors. After all, you can't eat out *every* night ... *or can you?*!

Food (Marketing) for People Who Hate Cooking

In 2017 Eddie Yoon, a director at The Cambridge Group and author of *Superconsumers*, released the results of a study he'd conducted on consumer attitudes toward cooking. Only 10% of the American respondents that he polled loved to cook, while 45% hated cooking and 45% were lukewarm about the activity. From this he concluded, "Beyond the numbers, it suggests that our fondness for Food TV has inspired us to watch more Food TV, and to want to eat more, but hasn't increased our desire to cook."[26]

Dozens of companies have been clocking this trend, and building solutions in response. Food kit delivery services have skyrocketed in popularity over the past five years, with companies like Blue Apron and HelloFresh leading the charge. A 2017 study by Packaged Facts brought these startling data to light:

- Nearly one-fifth (17%) of U.S. adults receive meal kits delivery services
- One-third (33%) of consumers familiar with meal kits have used free product trials
- Nearly all (97%) of meal kit delivery subscribers use the first company to which they signed up [27]

How did these companies become so successful so quickly? They spent big on marketing. Wanna know how much?

CAMPAIGN OF NOTE: Blue Apron, 2014 - Present

Blue Apron delivers boxes packed with fresh ingredients and chef-crafted recipes that guide subscribers through the process of making quick, easy meals at home. Founded by Culinary Institute of America-trained chef Matthew Wadiak, engineer Ilia Papas, and venture capitalist Matt Salzberg, Blue Apron was created to address a need that its founders were experiencing personally. "We liked trying new ingredients, new recipes, new techniques, but we found it really inaccessible to cook at home," Salzberg told *Business Insider* in a 2015 interview. "It was expensive, it was time-consuming, and it was difficult to find recipes that we trusted."[28] At first, the three co-founders boxed ingredients themselves out of their New York headquarters. Just four years later, Blue Apron was valued at $2 billion and had 4,000 employees selling 8 million meal kits each month.[29]

Although the company first launched in 2012, its multiplatform marketing blitz didn't begin in earnest until 2014. After a couple of years in the market, Blue Apron realized their concept had potential, but they needed to invest in a boatload of marketing to educate consumers on exactly how it worked properly.[30] To fund these campaigns, they spent $14 million in 2014, $51 million in 2015, and $144 million in 2016. In 2017, they started to scale back due to revenue hiccups ... but we'll get to that momentarily...

In addition to throwing heaps of money at marketing efforts, the company wisely leveraged a variety of innovative strategies simultaneously. They were early adopters in podcast advertising and absolutely blanketed that niche market with ads for several years running. They made sure their message was reaching a huge variety of potential customers by creating both online and offline campaigns. Blue Apron marketing messages hit network TV, YouTube channels, radio, display ads on popular websites, and consumer homes in the form of direct mail.[31] Finally, they created a phenomenally successful referral program that allowed current subscribers to send a free meal kit to a friend. In Blue Apron's S-1, the company stated, "Of our customers for the first quarter of 2017, 34% were acquired through our customer referral program." In that same quarter, referrals sucked up 14.75% of marketing spend,[32] but clearly, the company believed the ROI was worth it.

However, Blue Apron is not actually solvent. Not yet. This is due in no small part to their massive and ongoing marketing spends. In June of 2017, the *New York Times* reported, "Since its inception, Blue Apron has posted significant gains in sales, with its revenue in 2016 more than doubling from the previous year to $795.4 million. But it has continued to lose money — $54.9 million last year — as it has spent on marketing and growth."[33] And as other similar services began to flood the newly established food-kit market, Blue Apron was faced with a tough choice: continue investing in mega-marketing to differentiate itself, or scale back and risk losing market share to competitors.[34]

The company went public in June of 2017, raising $300 million, a full one-third less than it had hoped. Almost simultaneously, Amazon struck a deal to buy Whole Foods, sending ripples of fear through the entire food industry.[35] Business experts are struggling to predict exactly how these mergers, innovations, and sweeping changes in consumer desires will pan out, but they all agree that a revolution is in progress.

And that revolution is making grocery stores tremble: the death of home cooking would be a giant blow to the Tescos and Safeways of the world, and these legacy enterprises are scrambling to remain relevant. People are moving away from their kitchens in droves, and embracing a variety of convenience-focused eating solutions. GrubHub and UberEats now provide delivery service for restaurants that don't have the budget to pay their own drivers. HUNGRY, a workplace catering service, hires top chefs to prepare large-scale orders, then delivers them hot and ready to eat. All HUNGRY meals can be tailored to vegan, gluten-free, and paleodietary needs. Munchery offers a similar service—proprietary, healthy meals prepared off-site, then delivered—direct to single consumers. How we prepare and receive the food we consume is changing; for better or worse is yet to be seen.

Specialty Foods for Special Consumers

Grocery stores may be quaking in their boots, but they've got one-up on most restaurants and catering services: they can stock all the alterna-foods that massive global food producer Archer Daniels Midland cranks out. They've got plenty of room on the shelves for soy milk, buckwheat flour, tofurkey, and gluten-free-what-have-you. Restaurants have limited budgets for ingredients and can't reasonably maintain pantries that suit vegans, Whole30, and Alkaline eaters alongside their regular customers. And while we've pointed out that workplace caterer HUNGRY adjusts its menus to meet certain eating restrictions, it can't accommodate all requests for substitutions and special ingredients.

Too bad, since consumers are increasingly insistent that specialty food requests be honored anywhere and everywhere. Even in the face of mounting evidence that alternative ingredients can be unhealthy and horrendous for the environment.

Take coconut flour, a baking substitute beloved by gluten-free eaters. *Future Market Insights* reports that the global coconut flour market was valued at approximately $380 million in 2017, and is expected to soar to $720 million by 2027.[36] Even if you've never snarfed down a coconut flour-based cookie yourself, the hipsters in Brooklyn and aspiring actors in Burbank are putting 'em away with alarming speed. Other coconut-based alternative foods—namely coconut water and coconut oil, are also in high demand. This means the pressure on coconut growers to produce bumper crops season-over-season is increasing.

Coconuts are grown in the tropics, mainly in Indonesia, the Philippines, and India, with some additional farms in Brazil, Sri Lanka, and Thailand. Unless you actually live in one of those countries, your coconut flour took a very long trip before it arrived at your local supermarket, burning up loads of fossil fuels and blasting out carbon emissions as it traveled. Coconut groves aren't linked to horrifying deforestation like some other tropical crops, but the trees are often grown monoculturally, which depletes the soil of valuable nutrients and eventually makes it totally sterile. Toxic pesticides are used to protect nearly all non-organic coconut trees from hungry insects, and many of those pesticides pollute both air and water.[37] And, of course, the folks who grow and harvest coconuts aren't exactly billionaires: Fair Trade USA reports that farmers can make as little as 12 cents per coconut.[38] So that tiny $5 bag of coconut flour you bought to make some high-protein, paleo-friendly pancakes? It left a nasty mark on the world.

And yet many consumers plug their ears when presented with these facts because specialty foods *make people feel special*. Sauntering into a bakery, demanding gluten-free options, and storming out if they aren't available makes people feel superior, different, and important. And that, my friends, is marketing gold.

It's fun to make fun of alterna-foods but, of course, many of them were created so people with serious health issues could enjoy dishes that would otherwise kill them. Peanut allergies—which can cause hives, itching, swelling, wheezing, and life-threatening anaphylaxis—have been on the rise for decades. A 2017 study from the American College of Allergy, Asthma, and Immunology suggests that childhood peanut allergies have increased 21 percent since 2010.[39] And a childhood without peanut butter is hardly a childhood at all, right?

Enter almond butter, the slightly grainy but considerably less hazardous cousin to Skippy and Jif. Riding the wave of overall almond popularity—which has been fueled by high-protein diet trends and the never-ending American quest for guilt-free snack options[40]—this PB-wannabe has gained popularity for several decades running. Research consistently ranks almonds among the superfoods, touting the nut's ability to aid in weight loss, help prevent diabetes, and potentially ameliorate arthritis, inhibit cancer-cell growth, and decrease Alzheimer's risk.[41] No wonder people are ditching their jars of Peter Pan in droves.

Due to near-constant good press, almonds are widely believed to be the most nutritious nut available to consumers.[42] So even folks who *can* eat plain old peanut butter often *don't*, hoping to cash in on creamy flavor while consuming less saturated fat and more fiber. Almond butter is trendy, healthy, and a more evolved version of peanut butter. And oh, what a fantastic market position that attitude creates!

CAMPAIGN OF NOTE: MaraNatha, "Stages of a Breakup," 2017

In 2017 MaraNatha, a subsidiary of Hain Celestial Pantry that produces organic almond butter, partnered with boutique ad agency Terri & Sandy to create a campaign that leveraged the nut butter upstart's growing cachet. The campaign included a series of commercials that aired in 2017 on TV, in theaters, and online in digital and social media. The campaign featured a comically-heartbroken animated piece of toast with little arms and a face, smeared with jelly. Why the tears, little bread dude? His soul-crushing tears were because MaraNatha almond butter has dumped his ass, no longer needing gooey sweetness to feel complete. So much so, that each commercial closed out with the decidedly superior-sounding tagline, "MaraNatha: A taste so pure, it's too good for jelly."[43] A bit elitist, if you ask me.

The breakup-themed ads are sassy and tongue-in-cheek, of course, but also subtly snobbish. They're not aimed at chubby-cheeked kids with severe peanut allergies; they're aimed at health-conscious moms with big budgets. In fact, the only human featured in any of the commercials is a beautiful, slim young woman in workout togs eating MaraNatha almond butter straight from the jar. Terri & Sandy's campaign underlines the subtext of almond butter consumption, which is that people who choose almond butter over peanut butter are special. SO special.

As a side note, here are some of the alarming facts that oh-so-special consumers of almond butter (and almond milk, and almond flour, and ... well, you get the point) are studiously ignoring:

- Between 2005 and 2016, American demand for almonds grew by more than 220 percent[44]
- One almond requires 1.1 gallons of water to produce
- Eighty-two percent of the world's almonds come from California, a region that has battled crushing droughts over recent years[45]

Almond butter and other almond products aren't just costly to the environment; they're costly to consumers. In a searing article titled, "Lay Off the Almond Milk, You Ignorant Hipsters" *Mother Jones* agriculture correspondent Tom Philpott points out that, "A jug of almond milk containing roughly 39 cents worth of almonds, plus filtered water and additives, retails for $3.99."[46] If that inflation scale shocks you, brace yourself for this: In England, almonds and almond products are so popular they've doubled in cost over the past five years, and sales of almond milk increased 79 percent in a single year.[47]

Which sounds alarming, but may prove beneficial. After all, aren't wildly expensive things the special-est of all?

How do you make eating sexy? By making it exclusive.

Eating is one of the most mundane activities that humans engage in. It's no wonder then that marketers have manufactured messaging urging us to eat in finicky, highly specific, difficult-to-accommodate ways. How do you make eating sexy? By making it exclusive. Dairy, sugar, and flour are for the mundane, the unworthy. Superior beings crave weird, expensive, resource-greedy versions of those centuries-old cooking staples. Cool people shun gluten and embrace agave; exceptional people eat quinoa by the pound.

Clearly, specialty and alternative foods rise and fall alongside the dietary trends that tout them. And although those trends always claim to be rooted in groundbreaking health research, they're actually buoyed by our collective desire to lose weight FAST and look great NOW. And that collective desire is frequently thwarted by our cravings for tasty, highly-caloric, sweet treats. And don't marketers just know it.

Sweet Indulgences

Standing against the kale evangelists and turmeric latte-swillers, we have the disgruntled, stressed-out, sugar-addicted masses. These folks work long hours, battle insomnia, support large families, and haven't vacationed in years. Their hair is messy, their clothes are rumpled, and they are on their collective last nerve. "Eating healthy" seems like a worthy goal, but it's a goal that feels far out of reach, which makes this population highly susceptible to messaging about "treats" and "indulgences" and "rewards." They don't have the patience to wait around for the long-term payoff of a fancy raw food diet; they need something to make them feel good, like... RIGHT NOW.

Cadbury, Ben & Jerry's, Hershey's, and Sara Lee are more than happy to oblige.

A 2018 FONA International report revealed that 83% of consumers eat snacks daily, and 26% of those people snack to "treat or reward" themselves. The FONA study found that the vast majority of snackers (50%) tended toward "classic indulgence," which the organization defined as "treating yourself, sinful decadence, nothing healthy about it ... Guilty pleasures of choice after a long work week." Top classic indulgence snacks include chocolate, ice cream, cake, candy, and soda.[48]

Another 2018 study, conducted by a full-service food branding agency, Foodmix Marketing Communications, reveals that even self-professed healthy eaters will treat themselves to unhealthy food depending on how crappy they feel. 40% of Americans who described their daily diet as "extremely healthy" still agreed with the statement, "When I'm feeling down, I eat something indulgent to make me feel better."[49]

So, predictably, marketers of candy, ice cream, and other sweets lean hard on messaging that encourages consumers to take a break from dieting and shove some sugar into their ailing systems. They do this under a variety of guises.

KIT KAT: Since the mid-1980s, this distinctively designed candy bar has commanded consumers "Gimme a Break." The original jingle that accompanied this tagline promised that chowing down on a Kit Kat would "make your day," and many more recent commercials have portrayed people taking breaks from various types of work to treat themselves to a little chocolatey goodness. Although "Gimme a Break" clearly references Kit Kat's four-segment, breakable design and implies sharing your candy with others, the company consistently leverages the double-entendre to encompass resting, relaxing, and indulging, too.

OREO: In 2017, the beloved cookie company released the "Oreo Dunk Challenge," a campaign that focuses on the little rituals people create around eating the cookies, including twisting them apart, licking the filling, and dunking them in milk. The idea was spawned by a study showing that eating rituals help people savor and enjoy foods more fully,[50] and the ads were designed to show celebrities in the act of indulging in their favorite Oreo-eating prep routines.

SNICKERS: The "You're Not You When You're Hungry" campaign highlights situations in which people behave erratically due to extreme hunger, then return to normal after snarfing down a Snickers bar. This successful string of print and TV ads gets at the idea of "treating yourself" somewhat obliquely by implying that someone who has become hangry (hungry + angry,) should automatically reach for a candy bar to soothe their inner savage beast.[51]

While certain treat-centric brands have pinned their marketing strategies to the more G-rated aspects of indulgence, other purveyors of sugar-packed snacks have taken a racier route. Hundreds of years ago Aztec emperor Montezuma would feast on cocoa beans before hopping in bed with his paramours,[52] and ever since then, people have clung to the notion that chocolate is an aphrodisiac. Which means that campaigns linking sweets and sex are a bit of a no-brainer ... though some brands have taken the sensual connection further than others.

CAMPAIGN OF NOTE: Magnum Ice Cream, "For Pleasure Seekers," ongoing tagline

Magnum products have been sold in Europe since 1989 but didn't make their way to America until 2011. The company long relied on a relatively tame aspect of indulgence—exclusivity—by lauding its premium ingredients, including Madagascar-sourced vanilla and Belgian chocolate.[53] But for several decades, Magnum has built campaign after campaign on the tagline "For Pleasure Seekers," churning out accompanying visuals that range from the merely suggestive to the borderline softcore. A mid-1990s TV spot shows a woman approaching a man holding a Magnum ice cream bar, leaning down to lick it, and appearing to bystanders watching from across the street to be giving him.... the ultimate oral pleasure, shall we say? (It aired in Europe, of course.) Print ads throughout the 2000s showed scantily-clad women roiling on shag carpets while sensually biting their own thumbs, and fully nude couples cuddling, all with Magnum bars as props, of course. The company even nudged their sugar-coated-sex messaging into the twenty-first century with the "Be True to Your Pleasure" spinoff campaign featuring gender non-conforming individuals and a married lesbian couple.[54]

For the U.S. launch in 2011, Magnum released a splashy, stylish string of ads starring spokesperson Rachel Bilson and directed by fashion industry icon Karl Lagerfeld. Golin Harris*, the creative agency behind the spots, said, "When it came to launching in America, failure was not an option for the world's largest ice cream brand. Our strategy: "to sell pleasure, not ice cream."[55] (*The agency later rebranded and is now known as Golin.) Although the campaign threw luxury and style into the mix, the "For Pleasure Seekers" tagline accompanied every print, TV, and online ad.

Was it just a happy coincidence that Magnum already enjoyed a well-endowed reputation in America? In most American minds, the "Magnum" brand was firmly associated with larger-size condoms. No American in their right mind would link ice cream with "Magnum" unless they were planning an exceptionally sensual and sticky evening. But this was no deterrent to the European sweet manufacturer. Sex and sensuality were key to selling its wares, and in the (comparatively) uptight American landscape, the unintended link to prophylactics was a bonus. The luxury ice cream's titillating tagline made a stylish debut.

Clearly, brands selling sugary snacks embrace pusher-like narratives that imply, "Go on, you deserve this!" tempting hangry people by playing on their lack of self-control. On the other side of that coin, we find marketing directed at dieters that screams, "Lose weight or die lonely!" with the subtext of, "Don't you *dare* treat yourself, fatso!" These messages are often consumed back-to-back, but that self-control link binds them together. So next, let's sink our teeth into how eating and diet trends have been manipulated and marketed over the decades.

What Not to Eat

We may be able to blame the ancient Greeks for inventing restrictive eating, but there's no denying that Western culture has built a towering empire of rules, hierarchies, and diet-related maxims on that centuries-old foundation. That empire is a helluva money-maker. In fact, in early 2018, the diet and weight loss industry in the United States alone was valued at $70.3 billion.[56] A 2018 *Markets and Markets* report estimates that by 2022, it will have jumped to a staggering $246 billion.[57]

Of course, the word "diet" has become passé. Even though millions of people are trying desperately to lose weight, they've begun to shy away from the idea of dieting. In part, because dieting seems desperate, conformist, and like a low-level form of self-loathing. ("You don't think you're beautiful, just as you are? Are you broken inside or something?!") And in part, because people are finally starting to see that diets don't work.

Social and Health Psychology professor, Traci Mann, has known this for years.

Her work at the University of Minnesota's Mann Lab, and previously at UCLA, has focused on the psychology of weight loss and her two decades of research has consistently proven that dieting is a losing battle, simply because of how we're wired. She told NPR, "The focus of my work, from the beginning, was the self-control of eating. I was looking for ways to keep dieters from overeating. Slowly, over the years, I came to realize that nearly everything I studied (e.g., stress, distraction, and others) caused dieters to lose control of their eating, and it began to make sense to me why diets were so likely to fail."[58]

And yet, it seems like every few months a new way of eating—or group of foods that must be avoided at all costs—pops up. Weight Watchers and SlimFast still turn a profit, but with the new stigma associated with actual "dieting," they're wallflowers at the weight loss party. The new wave of diets promise so much more than just dropping dress-sizes; they claim they'll transform you, inside-and-out.

Those claims aren't coming from corporations peddling diet shakes or frozen meals; they're coming from gurus.

Modern diets are made popular by fitness buffs, nutritionists, and doctors who pen books filled with research, tips, and recipes. When a critical mass of social media influencers have followed their advice and dropped enough weight for some flashy before-and-after Instagram posts, those books start flying off the shelves. After a few talk show appearances, the world is on fire with whatever restrictive, flavorless, utterly unsustainable eating regimen the weight loss charlatan-of-the-moment is peddling.

Was that harsh? Sometimes the truth hurts.

How these folks choose to market their books and philosophies varies. Plenty of individuals steer clear of diet-related messaging altogether. Melissa and Dallas Hartwig, both certified sports nutritionists, wrote *The Whole30: The 30-Day Guide to Total Health and Food Freedom*, which has sold millions of copies. It only mentions weight loss on the back cover and generally steers clear of the d-word. Dr. Ian K. Smith's 2018 book *The Clean 20: 20 Foods, 20 Days, Total Transformation* took a similar route, leaving "diet" out of the title and lumping weight loss in with "disease prevention and overall health" as potential benefits in book descriptions. Others know that people might not want to admit they're dieting, but if they're looking for a new eating plan "diet" will top their list of search terms. Chef Amy Ramos' *The Complete Ketogenic Diet for Beginners* and Dr. Vincent Pedre's *Happy Gut: The Cleansing Program to Help You Lose Weight, Gain Energy, and Eliminate Pain* must've decided that search engine keywords trumped dieting stigma.

Dr. Mann finds this dance around dieting infuriating. In an April 2018 interview for FADS Marketing, she said, "Calling it a 'healthy lifestyle'? I'm super sick of that. They're literally swapping out the word because you're not supposed to say you're dieting. So, they can't market their diets as diets. But what are they doing? They're counting calories or points. It's just disingenuous."

She's right. The diet industry and the eating gurus who run it have a bad case of A-Rose-by-Any-Other-Name-Syndrome. Sure, they have a bad case of A-Rose-by-Any-Other-Name-Syndrome. Sure, they appeal to our modern sensibilities, leaning hard on health, longevity, and increased energy. And they find ways to pitch their ideas that pull on our self-righteousness. The Paleo diet is popular because of basic human desires; it feels good to say you've found a "new way of eating and living," especially one that's based on science and grounded in the origins of humanity. Clean eating appeals because the very basis of the name means if you aren't a part of the club, you're eating dirty. Going gluten-free means eliminating an entire category of processed, human-made, deeply-evil foods that allows you to do better—joining an elite group of eaters.

But they're all just weight-loss plans in the end. And the truth is you feel like you're fat, you want to belong, and hopping aboard whatever diet happens to be trending addresses both of those worries in tandem. This is what the marketers are counting on; they're just putting the product in different wrapping paper.

CAMPAIGN OF NOTE: Nutrisystem, 2018

In late 2017, Nutrisystem began gearing up for Diet Season. New Year's resolutions are a huge driver of sales for diet products, systems, and books, and this titan of the weight-loss industry announced that it would be branching out with three new sub-brands: Nutrisystem Turbo13, Nutrisystem Turbo for Men, and South Beach Diet for 2018.[59] Although these were simply tweaks to existing lines, the brand managed to scare up a surprisingly large amount of press for their "new strategy."

Unfortunately, the quasi-new brands didn't have the revenue-boosting impact Nutrisystem was hoping for. In fact, the company's stock tanked in early 2018. In late February of that year, stock prices were down as much as 29%.[60]

Why? Potentially because the company chose to air and print newish versions of the same old ads they'd been running for more than four years. You know the ones, with before shots of big-bellied people on the left and their live-action "after" photos schilling for Nutrisystem on the right. Or, B-list celebs like Marie Osmond and Melissa Joan Hart plugging the brand with all their meager might. These ads had proven consistently effective for years but fell flat as prospective dieters saw them for the zillionth time in January of 2018.[61] Even the company's CEO, Dawn Zier, described their campaign strategy as "fatigued."[62] It turns out; the "new year, new you" crowd doesn't just want to get healthy, they want to get healthy in new, exciting ways.

On the flip side, people can show a rebellious resistance to so-called healthy eating, especially if it feels forced.

"We ran an experiment where we labeled foods as 'healthy,' and it was a big turn-off," Dr. Mann says. "The weird thing about it was we labeled foods as 'healthy' that people already completely, totally know are healthy like an apple or a carrot. But that label made them want to eat it less, just highlighting the healthiness."

Dr. Mann and her researchers offered attendees at a conference two choices: a candy bar or a piece of fruit with a health-related sticker on it.

"We rotated through a lot of different labels. Calling something 'healthy' made people less likely to take it, and none of the others had a noticeable effect. 'Healthy,' though, made it actively worse," she told us. A Stanford study supports her findings, reporting that when veggies got pushy health-related labels ("wholesome beets") people passed, but when they got fancy, seductive names ("tangy lime-seasoned beets") diners were more apt to eat.[63] That's right, folks, when someone actively tells us that food *we already know is good for us* is "healthy," we refuse to eat it.

Sound crazy? In light of our health-obsessed culture, it might. And yet...

"Some studies show that 'healthy' and 'bad taste' tend to go together in your head," Dr. Mann points out. "So, when people see something labeled 'healthy,' they may think it's going to taste bad."

And they may be right. Does anyone actually enjoy the *flavor* of kale?

But another more powerful factor is good, old-fashioned self-control. While we love the idea of eating healthy all the time, the reality of doing so is simply too oppressive.

"The intention-behavior gap is something that psychologists have studied forever. You can intend to do something, but you don't necessarily do it," Dr. Mann explains. "There's a big gap between deciding to do something and it actually happening. And that's the problem. If there wasn't an intention-behavior gap, everyone would be doing all the healthy stuff. Everyone would be exercising and eating healthy because that's what most people intend to do. It's just very hard to do."

And we've come full circle. Why do diets fail? Because they're hard. Why do marketers keep creating new ones? Because we want to believe that we can lose weight and become brand-new, super-desirable versions of our old, chubby selves. Why do we keep buying into diets, even though they never seem to work? Because we're suckers. Optimistic, masochistic, suckers who firmly believe that getting skinny will fix all of our problems.

THE FUTURE OF FOOD (AND FOOD MARKETING)

Take a look back at the first sentence of this chapter. (I'll wait.)

Here's my prediction: we'll never get back to our own instincts when it comes to food. We can't control our own portions, because collectively we haven't landed on a middle path. We're either at one extreme or the other. Remember New York's ban on large soda sizes? The ban on sugary beverages larger than 16 ounces was thanks to impact remains. People essentially screamed, "Don't tell me what to do!" But guess what? When you go to the grocery store today, what do you see? Little quarter-size cans. Behold the tiny-ass bottle, because the system said, "You can't control yourself, but we'll figure it out, and we'll give you better options."

That's what'll happen with food. **We live in a world of extremes, and it's not sustainable**; from what we eat and drink to the very products that are marketed to us day in and day out. The future I see is based on a Buddhist idea called the Middle Path.[65] As marketers, we've been focusing on the extremes. We've been missing the marketing opportunity to focus on the profit and opportunities for good living in the middle.

When you think of the Middle Path, you don't have to know anything about Buddhism. Traditional Christian belief gives you the 10 Commandments and a whole lotta "you-better-not's." You know the drill: thou shalt not steal, thou shalt not commit adultery, thou shalt not do this or that. Well, the Eightfold Path of the Middle Way is the opposite. Instead of listing things you should avoid <*Cough* Extremes. *Cough*>, it provides a system of guideposts or goals to live by:

- The right viewpoint
- The right resolve
- The right speech
- The right conduct
- The right livelihood
- The right effort
- The right mindfulness
- The right state of mind

The big picture is, we've all been programmed as consumers, with a sense of fear driving our behaviors over time. On one side, consumers are buying into the high-priced, hyper-marketed appeal of specialty products: rice milk, pea protein, all organics, raw foods, and so on and so on...

On the other side of the plate, you've got a meat lover's pizza, super-sized meals at the drive-thru, restaurant serving-sizes that could feed a small family, sugar-laden blended coffees topped with mountains of whipped cream. And so on and so on, (you get the idea.)

Why do these two extremes even exist, when the middle space contains a larger mixture of individual tastes, patterns, preferences and buying habits? Because until the last decade, the PtB couldn't track those individual data points.

Please think about that some more.

The PtB couldn't develop intricate, individually-targeted marketing strategies until you started:

- Logging into websites that use cookies to track your browsing behavior
- Carrying a mobile device that tracks your location wherever you go
- Using apps that allow you to "check in" to locations, logging your patterns of travel by time and duration of stay
- Using store-based apps to create shopping lists, apply electronic coupons, and order products online or pre-pay before going to the actual store itself
- Researching and buying products online—revealing not only your budget preferences but also your tendency to buy based on recommendations and reviews
- And so much more

Not until you started providing those data points, were the PtB able to target anything between the two extremes. And we assumed that by targeting the outer reaches, those middle-path consumers would be picked up along the way by peer influence or coincidental overlap (because the message was in the right place at the right time to catch your attention.)

Come on back with me, back to "What's Next." What does this

mean for food, food trends and food marketing? As I said, marketers will have to take the lead, because as a society we've proven we can't make the right call on our own.

Watch for it, and you're going to see more blended products. Instead of plant-based or meat-based diets, meats will be blended with plant-based product. We **are** going to eat healthier because the system will divine the way for us.

Cows weren't meant to eat corn. They weren't meant to eat grains. They were meant to eat grasses, but you can't deplete the earth of its resources doing that. Solution: meet in the middle. The Middle Path combines a plant-based product mixed with actual beef, mixed with actual chicken, mixed with turkey. Guess what? That's less impact on the environment. That's less impact on farmers. At the end of the day, I'm still getting my vegetables. I'm still getting my meat. I'm still getting my protein (pea protein, in fact, has about 33 grams of protein in a 100-gram serving[66]).

The future of food and food marketing is this: stop living in the extremes. Meet in the middle for the good of our diets, for the wellness of our farming community, and for the future of our resources, water, land—all of these things.

We'll never be at a point where everybody eats plants, and we'll never be at a point where everybody eats meat. That's why marketers will be looking at companies working with pea proteins and other soy-based products, and figuring out how to market it to the masses in a way that reprograms our minds.

Here's the phrase again: behavior modification. We're on a mission to change your brain into believing that blended foods are the new healthy pattern and the truly sustainable way of health.

Do you want to play Devil's Advocate with me? Go ahead.

Why would marketers give a damn about a healthy way of life or sustainable food?

My answer is the same reason marketers care about anything: profit. When was the last time you saw almond milk cheaper than regular milk? That's right, *never*. When was the last time you found soy cheese cheaper than regular cheese? Again, never. It's always twice as much. There's ALSO enormous financial upside to offering the Middle Path.

It's already a strategy for restaurants and fast food. Look at all the ways soy is being used to extend food—textured soy protein is mixed in to extend hamburger meat; soy lecithin is used in frozen yogurt.[67] If the beef for a hamburger costs five dollars, the restaurant can blend it with soy flour and extend it into two patties. The result is a higher-protein product, more of it, at a reduced cost. That's where the profit is.

I'm not the only one who sees it this way. Look at True Food Kitchen[68] (locations in 12 states at the time of this publication). It's a restaurant that takes a balanced approach to food. You can eat vegan or vegetarian. You can get a turkey burger or a hamburger. You can get salmon. True Food is an interesting concept because it's smack dab in the middle so vegans, vegetarians, and meat-eaters alike can actually go in this environment and eat top quality of all three of those things.

Some of our most trusted trendsetters are also embracing it. In July 2018, media mogul Oprah Winfrey expanded her involvement in the world of healthy eating by investing in the True Food Kitchen.[69] She's quoted in the Hollywood Reporter, "I love bringing people together over a good meal. When I first dined at True Food Kitchen, I was so impressed with the team's passion for healthy eating, and of course, delicious food, that I knew I wanted to be a part of the company's future." *Wink, wink.* She wants to get in on some of that, but she's right. There aren't a lot of places where you can go and live the middle path in your eating.

Hold on; I see the Devil's Advocate has another point to make.

"You said it yourself—specialty foods are an extreme. They're high priced, and they appeal to a select range of people who can afford them. That's not a sustainable middle path."

That's right. But here's how it gets there: marketers will eventually use data and information and behavioral monitoring to determine if people are more accepting of blended nutrition. As we implement campaigns that reposition the blended product approach, it will become scalable, and more cost-effective. As more people buy into it, the cost will go down. It's the same thing you see around technology; the early adoption is highly expensive, but popularity makes it affordable.

Cost-effectiveness and profits, baby. Blended food products, ragingly-popular and made possible by *you*.

2

ALCOHOL

HAVE A SHOT OF THIS; IT'S ABOUT TO GET ROUGH

Revealing the mixology of alcohol, advertising,
and your hopelessly primitive brain

The Controlled Substances Act—passed in 1970 and amended approximately 3 trillion times since then—currently divides the items it regulates into five basic categories. According to the DEA, substances are put in certain categories (called "schedules") "based on whether they have a currently accepted medical use in treatment in the United States, their relative abuse potential, and the likelihood of causing dependence when abused."[70] So what are these schedules, exactly? Let me break it down for you:

	Potential for abuse	Accepted medical use in the United States (as determined by the federal government)	Safety (how easily people can become dependent on the drug)
Schedule 1 Drugs Examples: Heroin, LSD, marijuana	High potential	No medical use	Unsafe
Schedule 2 Drugs Examples: morphine, PCP, cocaine, methamphetamine	High potential	Medical use	Severe risk of dependence
Schedule 3 Drugs Examples: testosterone, codeine, hydrocodone with aspirin or Tylenol®	Lower potential	Medical use	Moderate or low risk of dependence
Schedule 4 Drugs Examples: Valium® and Xanax®	Relatively low potential	Medical use	Limited risk of dependence
Schedule 5 Drugs Examples: cough medicine with codeine	Relatively lower potential	Medical use	Limited risk of dependence

Alcohol is not a "controlled substance."

Mark Kleiman, a leading drug policy expert, and NYU public policy professor asserts that if alcohol were to be evaluated for controlled substance status today, it would fall under schedule 1 since it's widely abused, incredibly addictive, and has zero medical value.[71] And just so we're clear—take a look at the table again: schedule 1 is where you find HEROIN. The worst of the worst.

So why did legislators choose to exempt alcohol, a substance that destroys lives on an hourly basis, from strict government regulations? The simple answer is Money.

In 1970 when the act was passed, the average American consumed 74 quarts of beer, 3.2 quarts of spirits, and 5.3 quarts of wine.[72] That is *so much sauce*, people. And alcohol consumption had been rising steadily over the decades, so lawmakers saw the writing on the wall. If they kneecapped this powerful and popular industry, they'd never get re-elected. So, they gave booze a pass (along with tobacco) and allowed that industry to continue booming. And boom it did: the Beverage Information Group reported that alcoholic drink sales in the United States clocked in at $223.2 billion in 2016.[73]

You can bet some of that money is lining the pockets of modern-day congresspeople because booze peddlers continue to get a pass. Although alcoholic beverages can't be *sold* to anyone under the age of 21, makers of alcoholic beverages can market their products to *everyone*. And they do, through media that reach the eyes and ears of people far below the legal limit. The FTC doesn't regulate alcohol ads AT ALL,[74] which means the industry is trusted to self-regulate. (*Excuse me while I stifle a sardonic guffaw.*) Although some feeble and mostly PR-driven attempts are made to avoid actively marketing to tiny children, alcohol campaigns still blanket social media, radio stations, television, and websites, tempting both of-age and under-age drinkers to imbibe.

Further penetration is achieved via event sponsorships, where beer and booze brands encourage people to emotionally and automatically associate alcoholic products with their favorite hobbies and interests. Know who attends tent-littered, live-music-filled, outdoor weekend events? Families. Teens. Kids. They may not be the intended targets, but they still absorb the messages. Alcohol companies spend billions of dollars each year attempting to capture new customers, and multiple studies have shown that their marketing techniques have a substantial impact on teen drinking.[75]

But, ubiquitous as it is now, there was a time when alcohol marketing hit a massive lull. And, surprisingly, that time was when the industry was in the midst of a major renaissance.

Booze and Law: A Match Made in Hell

(Brace yourselves: short and snarky history lesson imminent.)

When the Volstead Act was repealed in 1933—thus ending Prohibition—an industry that had been forced underground was poised for a spectacular comeback. Manufacturers of beer, wine, and hard liquor could hardly wait to start *legally* selling their wares to all comers.

And yet, alcohol advertising after repeal was ... almost nonexistent. *Advertising Age* (a publication that was a mere three years old back in 1933) noted that "while the 14-year-old Prohibition dyke broke with a loud 'pop,' ... national advertising placed by distillers, importers or national sales agencies was extremely scarce, most of the copy which appeared having been placed by local retailers and dealers." What was THAT all about? Why on earth weren't booze companies flooding the airwaves and newspapers with marketing messages, clamoring for customers?

For one thing, they had no idea what people actually *wanted* to drink. During Prohibition, it was catch-as-catch-can; drink whatever's offered whenever it's handed to you. Whiskey was hard to come by, but homemade "bathtub" gin was everywhere. After more than a decade of drinking it, some Americans came to prefer it, especially women who found bourbon and Scotch too harsh.[76] Beer was popular in the immediate aftermath of repeal, but that might have been because it was one of the first alcoholic beverages to be made legal again.[77] And what about wine? Would everyone go on a binge, then settle down and become cultured lovers of Pinot Noir?[78] No one knew. And since it was 1933, they couldn't cook up a quick Facebook poll or perform some quick voice-of-customer research. So, no one threw dollars at costly campaigns; the industry waited and watched.

Another factor was that some state legislatures were quicker than others to approve the new regulations on liquor sales. A few companies played it safe to avoid placing ads in markets where drinking wasn't *actually* legal quite yet.[79]

But the main reason why repeal didn't launch a flood of alcohol marketing? Because alcohol producers were rusty. The entire industry was shut down by the U.S. government for 14 years, and once it had permission to start producing and selling again, it needed a minute to get its bearings.

Just imagine if all candy was suddenly banned nationwide, and federal Treasury Agents could arrest your local grocer for selling you a Snickers bar. (Side note: how on EARTH did the bozos who passed the Volstead Act settle on the Treasury Department as ideal enforcers? A true WTF moment in American history.) We'd all spend the ensuing years buying black market Skittles from dudes in dark alleys and finding non-candy ways to get our sugar fixes, while candy factories languished and candy companies folded. Once the candy ban was overturned, manufacturers would be far too busy trying to get their production and shipping processes back online to worry about cooking up ad copy. Recalibration would take time.

As it happened with booze, the government did some serious damage when they meddled with this industry, and the months and years of recovery from that meddling were filled with slow, resentful rebuilding.

Let's go out on a limb and say this is why the government has been so hands-off ever since. They passed a law that decimated a popular, profitable business; most people drank despite the dumb laws; legislators were reviled for making alcohol illegal; and when booze was back on its feet, its makers were considerably more prepared to defend themselves. Economists echoed the exasperation. Two years before Prohibition was repealed, a *Fortune* magazine article insisted, "The U.S. liquor industry ranks, in finances invested and in the volume of goods produced and consumed, with other great industries ... and should, rationally, be considered as one."[80]

Translation: Bourbon and rye are good for the economy, you D.C. louts. *Hands off our hooch.*

So, in 1970, hooch wasn't blacklisted in the Controlled Substances Act. And to this day, hooch-creators can market however they see fit. All because of a 14-year-long government blunder, the repercussions of which still reverberate through American culture today.

WHAT MARKETERS KNOW: DEEP-SEATED TASTES, TRIGGERS, AND THIRSTS

The people brewing up marketing campaigns for alcoholic beverages know that beer, wine, and liquor are all massive money-makers ...

and that beer, wine, and liquor are also products with huge behavioral and emotional impact on consumers. Let's ponder how they leverage gender, nostalgia, insecurity, and other vulnerabilities to get us drinking. And drunk.

GIRLS, BOYS, BOOZE

There's nothing inherently gendered about alcohol, but marketers have long believed that targeting *just men* or *just women* makes their work simpler and easier. (Wonder how they'll adapt when they finally accept gender fluidity. Panic? Denial? We shall see.) Gender targeting is the crudest form of customization: when a company says, "Hey, you're a dude. Dudes drink Jägermeister," your vulnerable, approval-seeking brain thinks, "I *AM* a dude! Obviously, I need to start drinking Jägermeister so other dudes will acknowledge my inherent dudeliness." All you have to be is male, and you feel included by male-centric marketing. All you have to want is to belong, and you're susceptible; crude but effective.

And, of course, most marketing firms don't actually whang potential customers over the head with gender-targeted messages. They insinuate, often leaning heavily on stereotypes that invoke broad, widely-accepted ideas about what a "real man" or "real woman" does, says, likes, and fears.

Take beer commercials. How many have you watched that DON'T feature a scantily-clad gal, buxom barmaid, or other overt objectification of women? If you happen to have beheld such a rare creature, it undoubtedly featured big trucks, men lifting heavy objects, and sportsball of some sort, all being enjoyed or enacted without a woman in sight. Because, for decades, beer companies have either relegated women to eye-candy status or totally ignored them as potential customers.[81] This is especially true of the beer commercials associated with sports broadcasts, a chauvinistic partnership born shortly after the 1947 World Series. Since then, marketers have paired beer and sexism so frequently and shamelessly that many blame this advertising trend for perpetuating the American myth that beer is a "man's drink."[82] Which, of course, means a *heterosexual* man's drink. (Wonder how they'll adapt when they finally acknowledge that gay people exist... and love beer, too.)

Of course, there have been some recent shifts in beer marketing, many of which appear to be driven by millennials, who are sick of both sexism *and* ads that glorify drunken frat parties.[83] But it's unlikely that the industry will ever truly eradicate the objectification of women. I mean, why ditch a tactic that makes so many beer-guzzling dudebros happy? No matter how trite, rudimentary, and overtly manipulative it may be?

But what about women drinkers? A JAMA Psychiatry study published in 2016—which surveyed tens of thousands of U.S. adults over the course of 11 years—showed that women are drinking more alcohol, and drinking it more frequently as the years tick by. (It also asserted that "problem drinking" has spiked among women, minorities, older adults, and poor people. *Why on EARTH would those people want to get drunk all the time, I wonder?*)[84] The report itself described these statistics as signaling a "public health crisis," but marketers took away a different message: time to shift strategies and target the fairer sex.

Instead of going the sexy-sex route they use for the guys, ad agencies the world over chose dark humor as their weapon of choice. Campaigns featuring exhausted moms chugging box wine to cope with stress, and women snuggling up to huge bottles of booze have begun surfacing on social media.[85] Underlying message: being a woman is the pits, but getting drunk off your ass might make it tolerable. Heavy drinking among women is being portrayed as a badge of honor, a sign of toughness. It's been both glorified and normalized because cashing in on this demographic has become a priority for beer and booze-makers and marketers.

But not all women-focused alcohol marketing campaigns tout binge-drinking or stress relief. And not all have led to phenomenal success. Let's look at two products, one that tanked and one that made millions because of women consumers.

CAMPAIGN OF NOTE: Zima, 1994 - 1996

Before we dive in, it's worth noting that Zima remained in production until October of 2008.[86] That's right, friends, this quintessentially '90s beverage limped along for 12 years after it became a global punchline. Not only that, in June of 2017, MillerCoors cashed in on a wave of 90s nostalgia by issuing a limited re-release of the clear malt beverage.[87] This announcement was met with an almost universal cry of, "Meh."

Oh, what a rocky history you've had, Zima.

But it's a history that included a brief heyday before a sharp decline. When Zima was first introduced, it was marketed to people who hated the taste of actual beer but wanted a drink with lower alcohol content than most hard liquors.[88] It was meant to be a bridge between bitter-but-macho beer and tasty-but-decidedly-NOT-macho wine coolers.

Back then "clear" stuff was all the rage; Crystal Pepsi, Mennen Crystal Clean Deodorant, Clearly Canadian, even transparent handbags crowded the shelves. Miller (not yet merged with Coors in '94) was the first bandwagon-jumper, filtering low-grade lager through charcoal to create a transparent brew. But the company foolishly dubbed their product "Clear Beer," and it was an unmitigated disaster. The clever folks at Coors knew that the inclusion of the word "beer" in the drink name was the killer: This was a new type of beverage that actual beer lovers would disdain since it lacked malt flavor and a foamy head, and that beer *haters* could embrace ... but *not if you told them it was beer!*[89] You suckers!

When Coors staged the nationwide rollout of its own clear malt beverage, Zima, in 1994, it did so strategically. (Well, *kinda.*) The television ads featured a shill in a black fedora who replaced all his S's with Z's and declared that Zima was "zomething different." He served as narrator and spokesman simultaneously, walking the viewer through scenes at bars and barbecues where beautiful people drank the clear brew happily from blue-labeled, fluted bottles. *Very high cheese factor.*

The clever twist was that the commercials purposely skirted the question of what, exactly, Zima really was, thereby upping its mystery persona. There's even a commercial in which the shill is at a bar flirting with a woman who asks him point-blank, "Zima ... what is that?" He denies both "beer" and "wine cooler," and instead of putting limiting labels on his beverage he just tells her, "Zee for yourzelf." (She, of course, loves it. FORESHADOWING!) Curiosity was piqued, the strategy paid off, and Coors estimated that 70 percent of America's regular drinkers tried a refreshing bottle of Zima in 1994 so that they could zee for themselves what the hell it was.[90] Good thing, too, since Coors sunk $38 million into promoting the beverage that year alone.

Initial sales figures were mind-blowing: 1.3 million barrels of Zima were sold in 1994.[91] But once that banked-on wave of curiosity petered out, the majority of drinkers returned to their old favorites, many claiming that Zima tasted metallic, overly sweet, or just plain gross. (Redditors have called it everything from "Scotch tape with lime" to "lemonade filtered through aluminum foil."[92]).

The exception: Young women drinkers. Although Coors marketing had targeted male drinkers who disliked beer but couldn't bring themselves to imbibe fruity Boone's Farm, the consumer base it had captured was ladies.

This was not ideal. This. Was. Not. The. Plan.

At the time, women drinkers were perceived to be less hardcore about their booze and comprised a much smaller potential audience than men. Not only that, Coors feared that if Zima became known as "a drink for girls," boys would reject it.[93]

They were right.

Journalist Brendan Koerner wrote an obituary/history of Zima when it was finally pulled from shelves in 2008, and opened his deeply entertaining piece for *Slate* with the following:

"There are a million ways to slight a rival's manhood, but to suggest that he enjoys Zima is one of the worst. Zima was the original 'malternative'—a family of alcoholic beverages that eventually came to include such abominations as Smirnoff Ice and Bacardi Silver—and it has long been considered the very opposite of macho: a drink that fragile coeds swill while giving each other pedicures." [94]

By 1995, Zima was in decline, and by 1996 the beverage's sales had fallen to a measly 403,000 barrels. Coors tried several formula tweaks and last-ditch marketing ploys to save the brand, including rolling out Zima Gold, which had higher alcohol content and an amber tint.[95] (So, um, it was beer.) But the damage was done. Zima was for girls, and that became its death knell.

Sure, sure, it stuck around in various formats until 2008 (and is still sold in Japan), and since it was cheap to produce yet could be marked up as a premium beverage, MillerCoors allowed it to linger. But it would never climb back to its initial lofty heights.

Why? Sexism, of course. It's socially acceptable for women to drink manly drinks, but social suicide for men to drink girly drinks.

It's a shame, too. In 2011, Gary Stibel, founder of the New

England Consulting Group, told the *Los Angeles Times* that women are responsible for 65% to 70% of the alcohol-purchasing decisions for at-home consumption.[96] Women may have boozed less than men in the 90s, but a 2013 study stated that binge drinking in women had risen 40% over the previous 16-year period.[97] In 2016, *Newsweek* pooled data from 68 studies in 36 countries with a total sample size of more than 4 million men and women across a time span of 100 years: Reporters found that although men had been more historically inclined to drink, by the year 2000 the genders were neck-and-neck.[98] (Not exactly the "gender gap" most women were aiming to close, mind you.)

Women are the new frontier when it comes to alcohol marketing, even if Zima couldn't hang on long enough to ride the wave of change.

There are some newcomers, however, who are more than happy to step up and cater their messages to lady-drinkers. Including...

CAMPAIGN OF NOTE: Skinnygirl® Cocktails, "Drink Like a Lady," 2012-2013

Back in 2009, reality TV star Bethenny Frankel began hawking Skinnygirl Margarita, a ready-to-serve, low-cal version of the classic drink. As of 2018, she's co-running the Skinnygirl Cocktails empire with Beam Suntory, Inc., and has expanded her offerings to include wines, naturally flavored vodkas, and pre-made mixed cocktails. (She's reported to have sold the brand in 2011 for $100 million,[99] although rather than settle for a lump sum, Frankel decided to receive ongoing payouts if Skinnygirl products sell well.[100] Clearly, she's in it for the long haul.)

In May of 2012, the brand launched a campaign titled, "Drink Like a Lady," which included tongue-in-cheek TV spots showing a prim retro-looking woman spouting platitudes about what a lady should do, interspersed with footage of modern women whooping it up while getting trashed. Skinnygirl still has the manifesto on the Cocktails site, which reads as follows:

"Ladies, it's time. Time to bring the old rules of cocktailing into the modern age. Time to re-write the books on the way we socialize. Time to redefine just what it means to be a lady. Sure, a lady always says, 'please' and 'thank you,' but a lady also knows what she wants, and isn't afraid to go out and get it. And Skinnygirl Cocktails is here to show you how. It's a woman's world out there, and it's time to Drink Like a Lady."[101]

Zima was ashamed to be liked by women. Skinnygirl has marketed to women, and only women, from day one. (And as seen in their manifesto, they're not above pandering.)

"It is important to know your message, identify your customer, and have a clear understanding of how to provide them what they need," Frankel told a *Forbes* reporter in 2016. "As a woman that sits in the bullseye of the demographic we reach, I feel like I have a sense of what women want."[102]

And, what women want are alcoholic beverages that are fruit-forward, cheap, and low in calories. After all, every woman ALIVE wishes she were skinnier. And simultaneously wishes that she could get totally wasted without worrying about her waistline. (See what I did there? It's so easy because that's how women are, right?)

The twist: some Skinnygirl products aren't actually that much lower in calories than their non-skinny competition.

- A 4-ounce Cosmopolitan averages 212 calories.[103] A 4-ounce Skinnygirl White Cranberry Cosmo will be about 100 calories.[104] Less than half, so definitely lives up to the hype.
- A 1.5-ounce serving of flavored vodka averages 90 calories.[105] A 1.5-ounce serving of Skinnygirl Vodka with Natural Flavors has 75 calories.[106] So a measly 15 calorie difference, and if you add additional mixers like fruit juice you up the calorie count even more.
- A 5-ounce glass of rosé averages 100 calories.[107] A 5-ounce glass of Skinnygirl Rosé will cost you ... 100 calories.[108] UH-OH.

The mixed drinks may be substantially skinnier than traditional cocktails, but the wines cut it mighty close. Most are between 15 and 20 calories lower per 5 ounces than non-reduced-calorie wine. But! As Paula Erickson, who worked as VP of Global Communications and Public Relations at Beam Inc. pointed out, Skinnygirl wines do "offer a stress-free experience for the modern wine consumer."[109] Whatever the hell THAT means.

Also worth noting: Skinnygirl wines are only 10 percent alcohol by volume, which slots them in below the 12 to 15 percent standard for regular wines. Skinnygirl vodkas are only 30 percent alcohol, compared to the industry standard 40 percent.[110] So even when Frankel's concoctions contain fewer calories overall, you'll need to pound a higher volume of liquid to feel the effects.

Based on this evidence, Skinnygirl Cocktails lead us to two painfully obvious conclusions:

1. Women are so obsessed with being skinny, you can slap the word "skinny" onto a borderline non-diet product, and they will buy it. (At least for a while: Skinnygirl was the fastest growing liquor brand in 2011[111], but has since been in steady decline.[112])
2. Proudly and cannily marketing booze directly to women drinkers... WORKS.

Of course, Skinnygirl isn't alone; many of the big guns have finally gotten the message that women want to feel included in drinking culture. 2015 saw Pendleton Whiskey assembling the Pendleton Posse, a group of tough, whiskey-drinking gals who travel around America, visiting seasonal festivals and events to plug the brand.[113] Anheuser-Busch jumped on board in 2017, speaking exclusively to women in their Lime-a-Rita™ campaign, "Make it a Margarita Moment."[114] In 2018 Johnnie Walker introduced us to "Jane Walker," a female version of their iconic Striding Man logo who graced a special edition of their Black Label blend. One dollar from every bottle sold was donated to charities that support gender equality.[115] After decades of exclusion, women are finally being recognized as the hard-drinking population they've always been.

Ahhh, how gratifying to witness the march of progress...or something.

Mainstream Alcohol Marketing Featuring Weirdos

Here's a gross generalization: most alcohol marketing targets the most normal of the normal. This allows brewers and distillers to reach the largest possible audience while simultaneously casting alcohol consumption as utterly commonplace and unquestionably cool. The exception, of course, is wine—which targets snobs ... but relatively normal snobs. Instead of niching, booze peddlers tend to aim for the lowest common denominator, which is everybody.

And yet, alcohol marketing occasionally takes a sharp turn into the deeply weird. This is especially true of beer commercials, which definitely tend toward sexist stereotypes but also have a history of dabbling in the surreal and nonsensical.

Consider the Budweiser "Whassup" campaign from 1999. Developed for Anheuser-Busch by DDB Worldwide Chicago, the centerpiece television ad features five young African-American men (already a departure from the brand's typical demographic) basically just enthusiastically and repeatedly saying "Whassup?" into the phone at one another. If you've never seen this commercial and have just read my description of it, you're probably thinking, "Uh, really? That's it? What's the point and what does it have to do with drinking a Bud?"

If you've EVER seen this commercial—even just once—you know it is one of the most hilarious, endearing, iconic TV spots in recent history. It's bizarre, goofy, and odd ... and somehow, it totally works.

"Four friends, 'watchin' the game, havin' a Bud' cut across all cultural barriers to become one of the most popular and memorable campaigns ever. It was one of the first campaigns to go viral," says Bob Scarpelli, former chairman and chief creative officer at DDB.[116]

He's right, though he's not giving you the whole story.

"Whassup" was a widely distributed, mainstream ad for one of the most popular beers in America that featured a minority cast ... but was NOT specifically directed at a minority audience.[117] It also utilized slang and cultural references drawn from African-American culture. Which all sounds extremely progressive and inclusive and forward-thinking, right? What Scarpelli *isn't* divulging is that Budweiser was a largely white company that had historically marketed to white men, and had strategically chosen to evoke the cachet of black culture in this campaign. Yes, black men might see it and experience relief at seeing themselves represented in a big-budget campaign, but what about white men? If they saw it and loved it (which many did), they probably didn't realize that this brand was co-opting a cultural phenomenon to make itself appear cooler, more modern, and edgier.

"Whassup" was bizarre and deeply enjoyable ... but not quite as random as it might've appeared on the surface. The DDB team saw an opportunity to appropriate an African-American slang term to make a somewhat stodgy beer brand seem current and less racist; a shrewd and calculated move.

Let's dissect a few more campaigns that seem harmlessly weird and quirky, but actually, work on the deep and hidden levels of our collective psyche.

CAMPAIGN OF NOTE: Bud Light, "Dilly Dilly," 2017-2018

You can thank the Wieden+Kennedy ad agency for this wildly-popular and deeply strange series. Launched at the beginning of American football season in August 2017, the first ad in the campaign shows the king of a medieval-style realm, sitting in a banquet hall and receiving gifts of Bud Light from his subjects. When they deposit their six-packs on his table, he declares each "a friend of the crown" and toasts them by saying, "dilly dilly." The whole hall responds, "dilly dilly!" But when some poor sap saunters in and offers "a spiced honey mead wine that I have really been into lately," they usher him out into the "pit of misery." *New York Times* reporter Daniel Victor concludes, "The implication is that Bud Light is for you and all of your friends; fancy craft beer is only for yourself."[118]

So undertones of alcohol-related camaraderie, but presented in a decidedly quirky package. An unexpected choice to push out during normal, basic, utterly mainstream football games.

But it caught on, and it became a meme. And as more "dilly dilly" ads began to circulate, more people started using the catchphrase. Sports fans especially embraced it, and soon bootleg "dilly dilly" jerseys, mugs, and bumper stickers began showing up. Then, in November, Pittsburgh Steelers quarterback Ben Roethlisberger hollered out "dilly dilly" during a fourth-quarter snap count,[119] and the deal was sealed.

But how? Why? Where did this wacky campaign come from? David Sutton, CEO of marketing firm TopRight Partners, hypothesized in an interview with INC Magazine:

"[Budweiser's parent company Anheuser-Busch] develops a creative brief that gives direction to the ad agency: What demographic you want to reach, what markets, what attributes...basically a how-to blueprint for who will drink Bud Light and how you can sell millions of cases. The agency says, 'What does that target audience do?' Well, many of them are watching Game of Thrones. 'What are the drinking occasions?' Well, many of them go to parties. So let's use a metaphor for something they already like: Game of Thrones. And let's speak to a common problem: If you're the host or you're a guest, what beer do you bring? That creates a lot of stress. So, let's solve that while speaking to the target audience. And let's have fun with it." [120]

Ads that may seem to be out of left field are actually rooted in strategy.

And yet the phrase itself is totally meaningless. Anheuser-Busch InBev Chief Marketing Officer at the time Miguel Patricio told *Business Insider*, "'Dilly Dilly' doesn't mean anything. That's the beauty of it. I think that we all need our moments of nonsense and fun."[121]

Clearly, the keyword here is "fun." Even if you don't get the "dilly dilly" ads, you instantly understand that they're meant to be goofy and lighthearted. You remember them much longer than you'd wish to... and that's the point.

CAMPAIGN OF NOTE: Dos Equis, "The Most Interesting Man in the World," 2006 - 2018

That's right, various iterations of this campaign have been around for 12 years. If that's not a mark of success, I don't know what is.

When first launched, "The Most Interesting Man in the World" campaign included several commercials showing a distinguished-looking gentleman with gray hair and a beard sitting alone in an oversized semi-circular bar booth; listing off his exploits. He humbly but confidently tells the camera, "I taught a horse to read my email for me" and "I almost broke the land speed record in 2008. Popular opinion amongst my team was that my beard caused too much wind resistance. I would have shaved it except ... *no, I wouldn't have.*"

He then explains how he came to be the spokesman for Dos Equis: "I fell in love with Dos Equis after my short stay in jail in Guadalajara. In fact, I returned every Thursday after I was sprung to play canasta with some of the guards." Makes sense, right?

Later iterations utilize an off-camera narrator who describes this man's accomplishments as reenactments; showing him at younger ages and through grainy, vintage-looking film. In a deep baritone voice he informs us, "His personality is so magnetic he is unable to carry credit cards," "He can speak French ... in Russian," and "He's a lover, not a fighter ... but he's also a fighter so don't get any ideas." The final shot in these spots is The Most Interesting Man himself at that same oversized booth, surrounded by cleavage-baring women, saying, "I don't always drink beer, but when I do ... I prefer Dos Equis."

A catchphrase which spawned approximately 3 trillion "I don't always *X*, but when I do ... I, *Y*" memes. Seriously, just ask the internet. Or, ask the actor who played him, Jonathan Goldsmith, who told *Esquire*, "I was told that I was the most meme'd person in the world!"[122]

Those memes paid out. In 2009, three years after the campaign first launched, most imported beers were losing market share to craft beers, with sales falling an average of 4%. Dos Equis was up 22% that year. USA Today reported that total brand growth between 2007 and 2016 was a whopping 34.8%.[123] Coincidence? Nope. In fact, in late 2016, the brand replaced the wildly-popular Goldsmith with a younger actor and sales plummeted. *Beer Business Daily* reported that Dos Equis was "off to a rather lousy start in 2018," citing data showing sales volume down 5.8 percent as of mid-February 2018.[124]

Where does this kooky subset of marketing campaigns fit into the larger scheme of alcohol advertising? What's the strategy behind tossing a few eccentric gems in among the commonplace, everyman messages?

1. **Acknowledge the outsiders:** If the goals are truly to encourage EVERYONE to guzzle, you have to throw the occasional bone to the geeks and freaks.
2. **Associate alcohol with laughter:** Know what drunk people do? Laugh. Sometimes hysterically. A booze commercial that makes you laugh reminds you how much fun it is to be drunk. Or just tipsy. Or even just physically present at your neighborhood dive bar, which just happens to serve booze.
3. **Tap guilty pleasures and buried desires:** "Dilly dilly," purposely aped Game of Thrones, and Game of Thrones

is a show that half the population watches proudly and the other half watches on the sly. Virtually all humans who see The Most Interesting Man in the World want to be him. Just a little.

How come none of the cowboys-and-pickups beer commercials ever go viral? Because they're forgettable. It's the ones with weirdos that we remember; what every marketer knows.

Everyone's Doing It (Selling Alcohol, That Is)

People have been getting drunk for ... well, basically forever. As soon as we figured out that fermented liquids made us loopy, we were ON-BOARD. Even booze *brands* have been around for ages. The Sudo-Honke company has been brewing sake since 1141, and Bushmills got their distilling license way back in 1608.[125] But the presence of venerable brands who've spent centuries honing their formulas and techniques hasn't kept a stampede of newcomers from crowding the market. Including a few that might surprise you.

<u>The Coca-Cola Company</u>: I mean, why not? After dominating the soft drink market since 1892, it's probably time for this behemoth to jump into hard beverages.

In February of 2018, an interview with Jorge Garduño, president of Coca-Cola's Japan business unit, appeared on the corporate website. In it, Garduño explained:

"We're also going to experiment with a product in a category known in Japan as Chu-Hi. This is a canned drink that includes alcohol; traditionally, it is made with a distilled beverage called shōchū and sparkling water, plus some flavoring. We haven't experimented in the low alcohol category before, but it's an example of how we continue to explore opportunities outside our core areas."[126]

Uh huh. Coke is edging its way toward alcohol production and distribution by tinkering with alcopop, a product with 3% to 8% alcohol, putting it in direct competition with beer.[127] The company will be rolling out its version of Chu-Hi exclusively in Japan with no plans to expand into other countries at the moment ... but we'll just see about that. A few months before Garduño's announcement, a Wells Fargo analyst released a report in which he speculated that Coke might shortly announce a move into alcoholic drinks.[128] Coca-Cola is an incredibly aggressive corporation. Starting with the acquisition of Minute Maid in 1960,[129] the company has cultivated a habit of market domination through the purchasing of its competition. Who's to say it won't start buying out distilleries in the next couple of decades? And with a marketing budget that averaged $4 billion per year between 2015 and 2017,[130] there's bound to be some I'd-Like-to-Buy-the-World-a-Coke-level shenanigans in store. But drunker.

Celebrities: Let's be clear: celebrity-backed tequilas, whiskeys, and wines are just shy of celebrity-backed perfume lines. The famous person in question undoubtedly consulted on the formulation and rubber-stamped the finished product, but probably didn't build the oak barrels or consult with the chemists. In fact, two of the most profitable alcohol brands backed by celebs didn't even invite the stars into the distilleries:

- Jay-Z bought out French champagne brand Armand de Brignac (a.k.a. Ace of Spades) in 2014,[131] and it is now one of the most valuable assets in his portfolio.[132]
- Sean Combs, a.k.a. Diddy, a.k.a. Brother Love has forged a

profit-sharing partnership with vodka brand Ciroc that
yanked the relatively unknown brand up to number two in
the premium vodka category.[133] Since the company's value
is climbing toward $100 million, his cut is undoubtedly
substantial.[134]

Both of these popular musicians leveraged their fame and media
exposure to flog their beverages of choice and made absolute bank on
their deals. Some of the most effective marketing in the world is done
on the sly, in music videos and song lyrics, convincing us that we can
cut off a chunk of Jay-Z's swagger for ourselves if we just start
drinking his champagne.

Of course, some celeb-booze brands are true pet projects. Actor
George Clooney and his friend Rande Gerber took a trip to Mexico
and decided they needed to create a tequila they could drink all day
without getting a hangover. Casamigos was launched in 2013 and sold
to Diageo Brands for a whopping $1 billion in 2017. Purportedly,
Clooney and Gerber still taste every batch of the tequila, which is
sold in 20 countries.[135] In this case, the marketing angle isn't simply
that a famous person likes, endorses, or owns the brand, it's that he's
personally involved in its creation and ongoing production. Who
knows if the claim is true, but it rings true enough to sell a helluva a
lot of tequila.

VIRTUALLY EVERYONE ELSE: If you live in a major American city,
you've probably noticed that your hometown is suddenly overflowing
with distilleries, craft breweries, and small-batch breweries. Which is
because the craft alcohol movement is absolutely booming. As liquor
laws loosen and zoning regulations change, many major metros are
being crowded with aspiring entrepreneurs peddling everything from
bitters to vodka to 45 trillion kinds of beer.

And consumers cannot get enough. Hometown hooch, small-batch liquor, and beer brewed by folks who've pulled themselves up by their bootstraps—all appeal to eager boozehounds and cocktail connoisseurs. (Especially younger ones.) Expectations of local bars have even shifted to include boutique brands, like Knob Creek Rye and Aviation American Gin.

Seattle-based bartender Andy McClellan has been slinging drinks since 2004 and has also served as an alcohol buyer for nine properties over the course of his career. Currently, he manages the bar at Sitka and Spruce, an upscale restaurant that specializes in locally sourced and foraged ingredients. So, as you can imagine, the man serves drinks to his fair share of opinionated millennial hipsters. McClellan has observed that the allure of small-batch beverages has become so culturally ingrained that many younger drinkers are more interested in backstory than flavor.

"For millennials, the narrative around the products is more important than the actual quality of the product itself," he says. "The narrative is the advertising campaign."

He points to Tito's Handmade Vodka as a prime example. The brand has been around since 1995 but is seeing a peak in popularity more than two decades later.

"It's really the story, it's the narrative that has made it so popular," McClellan explains. "It's the story of a guy, a self-made man who wanted to create a handcrafted vodka. Made in America, made in Texas. They paint it as this good old classic American story, you know? But it's all bullshit because the company does not handcraft the vodka. When you have a brand that's producing tens of thousands of cases of vodka every month, the volume they're kicking out of that product means it can't possibly be 'handcrafted.'"

And yet, the brand is still Tito's Handmade Vodka. The company tagline is "America's Original Craft Vodka." Tito's story is front-and-center on the sleek, modern company website. This vodka is so popular that consumers expect it to be on the back bar alongside Grey Goose and Smirnoff. DEMAND that it be available virtually everywhere. And its popularity is driven by a fable about a humble dude with a cute dog who just wanted to make amazing vodka.

Undoubtedly, back in the 90s, Tito made every bottle himself in the "old-fashioned pot still" that's still called out on the brand labels. But today, he does what thousands of "craft" liquor makers do: he buys in bulk and tinkers.

"There are large, food-grade companies here in the States that essentially make alcohol that you can buy. And then all you do is run it through your still," says McClellan. "You take this high-proof alcohol, run it through your own still, dilute it to 80 proof, and it's like, 'Boom, here is vodka. This is our handcrafted vodka.'"

A little like buying a cake mix, adding a few berries from your own garden, and calling it "homemade." McClellan points out that vodka producers aren't the only ones to go this route.

"Ninety percent of all rye whiskey that's made in the United States is made in Lawrenceburg, Indiana, in a single factory," he explains. The factory is owned by Midwest Grain Products (MGP) of Indiana.[136] "Rye is actually pretty hard to produce if you don't know what you're doing, or if you don't have the right factory equipment to make it. Companies or brands will then just purchase that rye whiskey from MGP, run it through their stills if they have stills, or they'll just put it in barrels and age it. Or they'll buy an aged product and bottle it themselves, and slap their own label on it."

Disappointed to hear that your favorite booze brand isn't as small-batch as you'd thought? You're not alone. But to slake the thirst of growing customer bases, many small brands are either buying bulk product or selling out to larger companies.

"The locals now are sad that their favorite little brewery now is distributed nationwide, so you can go into any 7-Eleven, and buy a six-pack of 10 Barrel Brewing Cucumber Sour Beer," McClellan says. "They're picking up a lot more customers, a lot more drinkers, but then they're also kind of leaving their local followers behind."

Brand expansion may create disenchanted fans, but such is the price of success. And it's a price many companies are more than willing to pay, according to the stats. The Brewers Association—a trade association representing small and independent American craft brewers—reported that although overall U.S. beer volume sales were down 1% in 2017, craft brewer sales continued to grow at a rate of 5% by volume. The organization further stated that due to steady growth, retail sales of craft brews now account for more than 23% of the $111.4 billion U.S. beer market.[137]

The American Craft Spirits Association asserts that in 2016, craft distilleries sold 6 million cases. In partnership with International Wine and Spirits Research, the organization found more than 1,280 active distilleries in the United States in that same year.[138] The market continues to grow at quite a clip, reaching $3 billion in sales in 2016, and growing at an annual growth rate of 25.0%.[139]

Will the Absolut Vodkas and Coronas, Jim Beams and Crown Royals of the world get run out of the business by bearded hipsters with copper kettles? Unlikely. But alcohol consumption is tied directly to socialization, and socialization is inextricable from trends. If the cool kids continually choose locally sourced hooch over cheap well/rail hooch, the market may shift. How will the heavy-hitters respond? How will they pivot their marketing strategies to recapture the attention of lost customers?

Let's discuss...

THE FUTURE OF ALCOHOL (AND ALCOHOL MARKETING)

Big reveal: I believe there's a Middle Path for alcohol. The extremes are easy to identify. On one side, behavior drives alcohol consumption. People *want* to feel uninhibited; they want to have fun. The other side is defined by teetotalism—complete personal abstinence from alcohol.

Right now, the middle path looks murky, but we're clearly headed there. We know alcohol isn't all that healthy for us, but no one wants to be a downer, and let's face it—a lot of non-alcoholic products taste like shit. Marketers have marketed awful alcohol products (ahem, clear malt beverage.) I believe the movement is towards non-alcoholic product, but it will be improved. The products will taste better, and they'll actually taste like alcohol.

Practically speaking, the middle path for alcohol is another blend like we saw with food. It's a marketing campaign that says, "Have your first drink, and make the next one a really decent non-alcoholic beverage of some sort." How do we pull that off? It starts with marketers and product developers creating better tasting alcohols because the key is reaching people who want to have fun, experience a little bit of buzz, and wish to avoid the bad decisions that come with drinking too much.

Did you hear the one about non-alcoholic beer? *It's like a vibrator without batteries... fills you up, but there's no buzz.* For the longest time, non-alcoholic product has been pretty cruddy. It tastes awful. Lite beer, on the other hand, feels like drinking water. The middle path is a quality product with great alcohol taste. Have your drink, but pair it with something that's non-alcoholic, actually tastes halfway decent, and doesn't make you the shittiest guy at the party.

Believe it or not, some companies are getting non-alcoholic beer right. I've spent a lot of time in Munich, and I can tell you the non-alcoholic beer sells just as good as a regular beer. People will actually drink a couple of really big beers, then some Paulaner Weizen-Radler N/A. Then they go to work... literally every day. Marketers will find a middle spot around beer and alcohol. At the same time, the products in these kinds of beers are good for farmers. Hops. Barley. The sustainable aspect is built right into the product.

Devil's Advocate, do you have a question?

"Do you honestly believe that's possible? People love getting drunk. People love being buzzed."

What percentage of people love being drunk when they hit say, 40-years-old?

And who has money to spend on premium product defining new trends? People 30-years-old and up. You're not going to see all of those people trying to maintain their jobs and households, getting drunk. (Who among us hasn't lamented we can't live like we're 18 anymore?) Bodies don't bounce back, and there's more at risk. So instead, they'll catch a buzz and follow it with a non-alcoholic drink to maintain their sanity on the other side.

What of craft brews? They'll augment into non-alcoholic craft cocktails. People want to celebrate together, and they want to be healthy. They also want to reduce their consumption mindfully, so marketers of these products along with microbrews will define and present the new category.

What about brandy, rum, vodka? Those brands will move into non-alcoholic versions as well if they don't already have them. There will be low- to no-alcohol versions of your favorite products. Sutter Home has been making wine for years, so they came up with free brew champagne. It's not cheap, but remember we're still in that early adoption phase where prices are high. When the middle ground comes into play, the sommeliers will see it, the wine snobs will claim it, and we'll call it a new movement. Marketers have to change the pattern, and they're going to lead with products like these.

Here is another sign that the blended path is on its way to the masses: your local Walgreens stocks N/A product right next to the alcoholic stuff, and you can go to Amazon.com and order non-alcoholic beverages. If AMAZON will ship it to your house, there's profit in it. If Walgreens is selling it in stores, there's profit in it. Everyone else, from manufacturers to marketers alike, will get the hint. FAST.

Drinking and driving is the extreme, and abstinence from alcohol is the other. What's in the middle? Responsible consumption's in the middle. Even MADD – Mothers Against Drunk Drivers — has figured out that marketers are the key to behavior modification. It's right here in a 2014 press release:[140]

"MADD Virgin Drinks were conceived and developed by Hill Street Marketing Inc., to support Mothers Against Drunk Driving (MADD), both philosophically and financially. They're intended to provide adults 21 and over with an alternative to alcohol, and in

doing so, generate donations to MADD, the nation's largest non-profit organization working to protect families from drunk driving and underage drinking. We are excited to team up with Walgreens, the nation's largest drugstore chain, to reach health and safety-conscious American consumers," said Brian Bolshin, President & CEO of MADD Virgin Drinks.

Trust me. You're going to see more about MADD Virgin Drinks. You're going to see more collaborations. The future is a collaboration between distilleries and social drivers like MADD, getting together and creating a co-branded product.

That's my point. The future is about marketers figuring out a way for you to enjoy yourself and drink responsibly. The Middle Path will be non-alcoholic beverages blending into your drinking lifestyle.

No one wants to be the drunk that goes back to the office and has everyone talking. With marketers stepping in, they may not have to experience that shame.

INTERLUDE

SPECIAL CONTRIBUTOR JOY T. HARRIS

FADS MARKETING™

GOES TO VEGAS

FADS GOES TO VEGAS

Sin City! Viva Las Vegas! What happens in Vegas stays in Vegas! If ever there was a big, black, beating heart of FADS activity, it's this teeming Nevada metropolis.

The Las Vegas Strip, a 4.5-mile stretch of hotels and casinos, has been marketed as an adult playland for more than 80 years, offering up every type of entertainment and indulgence imaginable. (Along with a few that most folks could never imagine. At least, not without help.) No other single location in the United States is more driven by the successful marketing of food, alcohol, drugs, and sex. From billion-calorie-buffets to free-flowing booze, to stripper cards handed to tourists on the street, marketing of FADS is both prevalent and well-executed. And let's not kid ourselves: this Mecca of overindulgence is a microcosm of the entire United States.

While most products marketed to consumers target a specific niche, Las Vegas marketing crosses all socioeconomic levels. From the obscenely-rich to folks on a budget (with the most sophisticated of tastes,) to those who'll take what they can get, everyone loves to party with the masses in Vegas. Las Vegas offers food, alcohol, drugs, and sex in abundance to all visitors—so long as their money is green. Because there—unlike virtually everywhere else—the things we've been taught are "bad for us" are excused. Embraced, even! Indulgence is encouraged. Pleasure is painted as a God-given right. Las Vegas-based marketing flat-out tells us to eat, drink, and be merry ... and that all will be forgotten and forgiven when you pack your bags and head home. Sin City lures us in and once we're there, gives a little tug and sets the hook deeper.

And throngs of eager Americans are more than happy to be caught—like fish on a line.

Food Marketing, Vegas Style

The Vegas strip offers some of the finest dining in America, alongside some of the country's cheapest eats. No matter your palate, you'll find something delicious or decadent to suit your appetite. The hipster snobs would never want to admit it, but this place is a bona fide "foodie" paradise.

And a democratic one at that! High rollers can tuck into a $5,000 burger at Fleur by Hubert Kelly comprised of Wagyu beef, foie gras, and truffles served with a 25-year-old bottle of French red wine. Dirt-poor fortune-seekers can order up the famous steak dinner at Ellis Island for just $7.99. Not to mention the bountiful all-you-can-eat buffets found in every hotel on the Strip where gamblers can indulge in an endless variety of dishes. Every type of consumable is marketed to every type of consumer.

Restaurant food sales in 1970 totaled a mere $42.8 billion.[141] In 2017, they crested $799 billion.[142] That same year, the highest-grossing restaurant in the nation was TAO® Las Vegas, which raked in a cool $42.4 million.[143] No wonder marketers are having a field day luring hungry patrons into packed Las Vegas eateries.

Eat with Famous People!

The cult of the celebrity chef is alive and well in America—nowhere more so than Vegas. The marketing firms that advise these skilled cooks know that slapping a TV-approved name on a restaurant practically guarantees its success. You'll find eateries helmed by Bobby Flay, Gordon Ramsay, Emeril Lagasse, Wolfgang Puck, Nobu Matsuhisa, and Guy Fieri, to name a few. Of course, the celebs in question are seldom actually on-site ... but never mind *that*. Their names are on the door! They've approved the menus! Who cares if they've never actually cooked food in the world-class kitchens with their own hands! JUST EAT!

Back when Julia Child and Jacques Pépin ran the game, TV chefs made their money from cookbooks, speaking engagements, and on-air salaries. But with the explosion of competition shows like Chopped, Iron Chef, and Hell's Kitchen, celebrity chefs are both more common and more powerful than ever. As *Time* magazine asserted way back in 2010, "In the Food Network era, the phenomenon of the celebrity chef has utterly transformed the restaurant industry and, in the process, changed the very nature of how we eat."[144] Cooking shows increasingly convince us that we can't possibly be skilled enough to cook for ourselves, and subsequently that the best food available is anything rubber-stamped by a show-hosting chef. Seven of the top 10 highest-earning celebrity chefs in the world have restaurants in Vegas,[145] and their famous names alone are often enough to tempt tourists.

Easiest marketing in the world.

At least, if you don't count the infinite person-hours poured into writing, editing, and producing their TV shows; coordinating their tour and press schedules; writing their cookbooks; promoting their bodies of work, and wrangling their outsized personalities. So, maybe not THAT easy ...

Eat to Brag!

Thinking of food as sustenance is so passé. In the modern eating era, it's all about how your meal plays on Instagram and how weird/exclusive/dangerous the component foods might be. Documenting meals has become a national pastime, "food porn" is a real phenomenon, and people of all generations are proudly labeling themselves as "foodies." Eating isn't about eating any more; it's about entertainment, enjoyment, and bragging rights.

You can craft your own bragging-rights eat-a-thon by downing soup dumplings at China Mama, chicken-fried lobster at Binion's Ranch Steakhouse, and foie gras custard "brûlée" at Sage.[146]

Or you can plan your trip around the Bon Appetit-sponsored Uncork'd, an annual three-day culinary and wine event developed by the Las Vegas Convention and Visitors Authority in partnership with their advertising agency, R&R Partners. The 2018 lineup included master classes with Gordon Ramsay and Nobu Matsuhisa, coffee and cake with Giada De Laurentiis, cocktail classes with bartenders from the Venetian and Palazzo, and a steak-and-egg breakfast cooked for you by Wolfgang Puck... among others.[147]

Or you can book a Lip-Smacking Foodie Tour that will whisk you through multiple, mega-famous restaurants, sampling everything from escargot at Bardot to pickled lotus root at Yusho to bean-to-bar chocolate at Hexx.[148]

Take your pick, then take your pics. And Instagram the hell outta your Vegas vacay.

With that in mind, marketers have set up Las Vegas as an eating destination. The glut of indulgent restaurants are pitched as a solid reason to book a plane ticket, and Vegas vacations are painted as "food adventures." Many cities are defined by their local fare: deep-dish pizza in Chicago, lobster in Maine, Po' boys in New Orleans. Las Vegas may not have a signature dish, but it doesn't need one. It has something else in spades; top-notch versions of everyone else's.

ALCOHOL MARKETING, VEGAS STYLE

Aside from gambling, no pastime better defines Las Vegas than drinking. The city is famous for its lax alcohol laws, which draw millions of visitors eager to imbibe publicly without the threat of arrest. It's one of few places in America where public drinking is allowed. For many, a visit to Sin City is all about "getting your drink on."

As with food, Las Vegas marketers push liquor's appeal across the entire socioeconomic spectrum. Nightclubs have tried to outdo one another by mixing up breathtakingly expensive cocktails: the Wynn's XS Nightclub offers the Ono, a multi-drink cocktail service that runs $10,000 per couple, although that price tag includes a side order of his-and-her jewelry. You could also consider booking Hakkasan's $500,000 New Year Eve's champagne package which includes the world's largest bottle of champagne and personal serving staff of 40. But budget-conscious boozehounds aren't ignored; Penny-pinchers can hit up a $20 all-you-can-drink happy hour or stroll the Strip sipping on a 40-ounce frozen and fun-colored fruity concoction. It's all alcohol, all the time in Vegas whether you're drinking on a dime or drowning in cash.

Drinking Holidays!

I'm not just talking about champagne on New Year's Eve or green beer on St. Pat's. To maintain its rep as the city of excess, Vegas-based bars and casinos have started to market lesser holidays and minor life events as excuses to binge-drink until you black out.

It's Cinco de Mayo, a holiday that only holds significance for people of Mexican descent! Let's ALL celebrate with margaritas and tequila! It's Mardi Gras in New Orleans! Let's drink ourselves sick in Vegas! It's SUNDAY! Time for a boozy brunch replete with mimosas and bloody marys! While this event-based alcohol marketing isn't unique to Las Vegas, it is pushed harder here than anywhere else. Bars, restaurants, hotels, and casinos know that their city's lackadaisical attitude toward drinking and drunkenness are major draws and that they only need to create an easy excuse to tempt visitors.

DRINKING NOVELTIES!

Again, marketers the world over know that weird and outrageous drinks will always attract the fun-loving drinker. But Las Vegas takes this tradition to the next level.

For starters, bars across the city honor the Scorpion Bowl, invented in Hawaii in the 1930s,[149] with massive, shareable cocktails. For a measly $55 you can get a 6-person Moscow Mule at Park on Fremont,[150] or if you've got $80 to spare swing by Fiddlestix for an 8-person boozy milkshake spiked with deep-fried Oreos.[151] Hundreds of Vegas bars and eateries offer ridiculously outsized drinks and market them to groups of tourists looking to have fun and get wrecked.

Or if size doesn't thrill you, consider liquor in innovative new formats. In 2017, a handful of Las Vegas hot spots began selling Buzz Pop Cocktails, a deeply boozy push-pop frozen treat with about 15% alcohol by volume. The company was founded and is based in Vegas, and churns out Buzz Pops using fresh fruits and premium liquors. Suck on Mango Passion Fruit, Lemon Drop Martini, or Moscow Mule-flavored pops and get just as drunk as you would drinking them.[152]

Still not phased? How about a frosty mug of bespoke beer? Okay, you can only get this brew—described by makers Tenaya Creek Brewery as a mix between a pale ale and an IPA—at promotional events thrown by the Las Vegas Convention and Visitors Authority. But the beer was created and launched as part of the "What Happens Here, Stays Here" marketing campaign, and aptly named #WHHSH. What better way to promote Vegas's boozy culture than a buzzy beer with a hashtag for a name?[153]

Drug Marketing, Vegas Style

When you think about drugs in Las Vegas, you may think about illegal drugs and illicit substances, and those are certainly available through all the usual nefarious channels. But the predominant drugs —and the ones that are most heavily marketed—are the legal ones. The ones anyone can buy at a pharmacy. Or a coffee shop. Or a candy store. Vegas is one giant pharmacy, open for the liberal sale of mood-altering chemicals.

Along the Las Vegas Strip, you'll see a CVS or Walgreens on every block. Why? Because millions of travelers need to be within reach of their prescriptions and over-the-counter drugs. Also, hangover remedies and morning-after-pills are in high demand, and abundant chain drug stores are positioned to reach vast numbers of their demographics trolling the Strip. We live in a time where there's a pill for everything, easy access means more frequent purchase and consumption.

Drug Yourself Beautiful!

A class of drugs that's legal, pricey, coveted, and widely available to Vegas visitors? Injectables. Whether you want your forehead tightened with a shot of Botox or your lips plumped up with a bit of Juvéderm, an impressive fleet of medi-spas are there to serve you. The Cosmopolitan, Venetian, and MGM Grand have injection-ready spas within casino grounds, and the Strip boasts dozens more. Why not shave off a few years or a few pounds or a few wrinkles while you whoop it up in Sin City?

Drug Yourself Silly!

Sugar used to be a treat for kids, but now makers of candy and baked-goods are targeting adults. Both scientists and marketers know that a little hit of sugar instantly makes people feel good, and consequently, we've seen a huge increase in marketing sugary products to adults. However, "grown-up" sugar is more expensive since grown-ups have access to more disposable income. And since processed sugar is addictive and stimulates the same pleasure centers of the brain as cocaine or heroin,[154] sweet adult treats are a marketer's dream come true.

Whatever your poison, Vegas can set you up ... but why not get high on something tastier, cheaper, and safer instead?

Sex Marketing, Vegas Style

Nudes! Topless dancers! Strippers! Like nowhere else in America, sex is abundantly for sale in Las Vegas. The city is nestled in the only state in the union in which prostitution and solicitation are legal. Of course, they're only legal in counties with less than 400,000 residents,[155] so much of the action available in Vegas proper is of the look-don't-touch-type. But that doesn't mean establishments on the fringes can't come into the city to market their services. And they DO.

Sex Fliers!

During the 1990s, Las Vegas made a failed attempt to transform itself into a clean, cheerful, family-friendly tourist destination ... but by the early 2000s, it had given up on THAT malarkey.[156] Now that sin is firmly back in Sin City, brothels have returned to an age-old and highly-confrontational marketing tactic: barkers.

If you're sightseeing along the Strip, you *will* be forcibly-handed a playing-card-size "flier" featuring pornographic images of women, and all the info you need to find them in person. The folks hired to distribute these materials generally avoid anyone who looks underage or has actual children in tow—everyone else is fair game. While strip clubs abound within city limits, actual sex work must take place in low-population areas, so the fliers generally direct recipients to rural and suburban locales for getting down and dirty.

Physical fliers may seem prehistoric as marketing strategies go, and they are. But paper takeaways featuring scantily-clad images combine shock value, memorability, and titillation for a cocktail (pun intended) of consumer reaction that gets results. If it ain't broke ...

SEX SERVICES FOR WOMEN!

Wait, hold the phone. Women like sex, too?! And they respond to shows, and sex workers who cater to their needs? <pearl clutching intensifies>

This may be news to the general populace, but the shrewd people running the Las Vegas sex industry have been in on the secret for quite a while now. As women's sexual needs finally begin to rise to the surface in pop culture, male strip shows have gone from crude jokes to big business. Thunder from Down Under at Excalibur—a 75-minute highly "interactive" show featuring hunky fellas from Australia[157]—has supplanted the old-school gyrations of Chippendale's as ladies' choice. Actor Channing Tatum's "Magic Mike" movies (which are largely autobiographical, in case you missed that juicy tidbit) have been parlayed into a wildly popular, consistent moneymaker for Club Domina. The show runs five days a week, and front row seats will set you back $159.[158]

Up until 2010, male prostitution was technically illegal due to a loophole: sex workers in Nevada were required to undergo frequent cervical testing for sexually transmitted infections, and, crazily-enough, guys lack cervixes. But when the state health board finally approved a regulation to allow urethral testing for men, the game changed.[159] In an interview with GQ, Nevada's first legal gigolo said, "Women don't pay for sex, they pay for the experience. And luckily for me, I don't have that much experience with sex, but I have the mentality and the emotion and gumption to make them feel the way they want to feel."[160] (Working by the name "Markus," the history-making male prostitute made his debut at the Shady Lady Ranch, but left after a grueling two months servicing less than ten customers.)

Skilled male sex workers at various brothels may opt to work with both women and men, and women who prefer women are welcomed by many female sex workers. But most of the local women-focused offerings are tailored to the hetero-crowd. Regardless, Las Vegas' open acknowledgment of women's sexual fantasies, desires, and needs still seems remarkably progressive.

What happens in Vegas...maybe it shouldn't stay there, after all. I'm just saying.

3

DRUGS

LOOKS LIKE YOU NEED SOMETHING STRONGER

Mainlining the facts about drug advertising and your fatal inadequacies

Know what I love? When companies sitting on mountains of cash throw temper-tantrums over the consumer's "right to know" about their products. When corporations manufacturing controlled, potentially dangerous substances insist that regular folks can make their own decisions about how their health is managed. When behavior manipulation is presented as public service. LOVE THAT. So happy to live in a modern, enlightened era in which pharmaceutical megacorps are looking out for the little guy. And telling the little guy to ask his doctor about Lunesta.

Quick reminder: drug companies didn't always market directly to consumers in the United States. (And, aside from New Zealand, they're not allowed to market directly to consumers anywhere else at all.) Up until the 1980s, companies communicated with doctors and pharmacists almost exclusively,[161] trusting actual, trained professionals to consult with patients about their medication choices. Then, as American culture began to morph and patients demanded a more active role in treatment decisions, print and TV ads for prescription meds began to appear.[162] Today, of course, they're as common as ads for Taco Bell and Target.

Of course, it's worth noting that marketing prescription drugs directly to consumers was *never actually illegal* in the United States. Regulatory legislation passed in 1969 stipulated that any drug advertisements must hit four rudimentary marks:

1. They must not be false or misleading. (No lies.)
2. They must present a "fair balance" of information describing both the risks and benefits of a drug. (No sugar-coating.)
3. They must include facts that are "material" to the product's advertised uses. (No ... inserting random facts about random stuff? Like that the human head weighs eight pounds?)
4. They must include a "summary" that mentions every risk described in the product's labeling. (No masking the hazards. Which accounts for the ridiculously rushed, auctioneer-style list of ghastly side-effects tacked onto EVERY drug ad ever.)[163]

And that's it. Four loose guidelines. As was the case with the alcohol industry, the U.S. Government recognized that the pharmaceutical industry was loaded and powerful, and decided it was much safer (and likely profitable) to stand down. And, as was the case with alcohol marketing, the industry was largely trusted to make the right moral choices and simply self-regulate.

And for many decades, it did.

Until it didn't.

Because why the hell shouldn't multi-billion-dollar pharmaceutical companies be able to tell uninformed consumers about pills that will make them thin, virile, strong, and happy? Why shouldn't people with zero medical training be entrusted to pick their own meds, and demand them from doctors? (Doctors who are paid off by those same multi-billion-dollar pharmaceutical companies for their "support."[164]) Why shouldn't the pharmaceutical industry take Ralph Nader's crusade for prescription drug labels that warn patients of potential risks, and twist it into a larger crusade to ensure that drug consumers were "aware" of all their drug-taking options?[165]

Drug manufacturers poured $6.1 billion into direct-to-consumer marketing across television, magazine, digital, newspaper, radio, and out-of-home advertising in 2017 ALONE.[166] But, clearly, they did that for our own good.

The National Conference of State Legislatures reported way back in 2000 that sales of the top 50 most heavily advertised drugs rose 24.6 percent that year, compared to 4.3 percent for all other drugs combined.[167] But, clearly, drug companies just wanted us to know about our options.

Critics of direct-to-consumer pharmaceutical ads argue that they can trick consumers into demanding drugs they don't actually need from their harried physicians. And, taking the logic a step further, these marketing campaigns knowingly transform normal human experiences (hair loss, occasional insomnia, shyness) into fearful "diseases" that merit drug-based treatment.[168] This phenomenon is so widespread that it's earned the sinister name "disease mongering." But, clearly, we just didn't realize how much we *needed* those drugs until we learned about them. You know, through ads.

Of course, you knew this already. You knew that Big Pharma has been pulling our strings and playing on our insecurities for decades. No surprise there.

The newsflash is this: now, Big Pharma is digging deep into gamification and customization of its marketing efforts to make its ads even more effective. (Read: manipulative.) Now, Big Pharma is hiring behavioral scientists to work on its campaigns.[169] Now, Big Pharma is pushing for permission to market off-label drug uses; uses for which a drug wasn't originally formulated and for which it may not be fully tested.[170]

Now, it's getting serious.

WHAT MARKETERS KNOW: WE LOVE A QUICK FIX

Drugs that treat life-threatening conditions appeal to us because they keep the Grim Reaper at bay. Drugs that treat wrinkles and weight gain and erectile dysfunction appeal to us because they offer fast-acting, virtually effort-free solutions to our pesky "health" issues. Why eat less or accept that you're getting older, when you could inject or consume a substance that will fix you right up?

People love drugs because they hate work.

Speaking of things people hate to do, that extends to following a doctor's orders and taking medications exactly as prescribed. It's why the pharmaceutical industry had to turn treatment into a game.

Have fun, do drugs

In case you think I'm peddling conspiracy theory, here, allow me to cite a source. Healthcare reporter Kevin McCaffrey's 2017 piece for *Medical Marketing & Media* titled "How Pharma Marketers are Using Behavioral Science" included the following assertion:

"New technology has shifted the marketing paradigm from one-way messaging and simple reminders paired with education efforts to a new set of tools including gamification, augmented and virtual reality, and online interventions tailored to individual patients. Designed right, these advances stand to have a more meaningful impact: helping foster long-term behavior change to support brand objectives."[171]

Did reading that give you chills? Me too. Kevin told us that Big Pharma marketing departments are *already* leveraging cutting-edge tech to change how people act, nudging them toward behaviors that earn dividends for drug companies. Welcome to the future, people.

Of course, the companies themselves would argue that their interest is in patient well-being and sustainable long-term care. And it's certainly true that, at least when it comes to gamification, the primary motivator appears to be, "Get actual sick people to take their meds." But let's dig a bit deeper, shall we?

CAMPAIGN OF NOTE: SaxendaCare support program, 2016

Novo Nordisk hired healthcare marketing agency MicroMass to create a support system for patients taking Saxenda, a weight-loss drug and reformulation of its wildly popular diabetes drug Victoza. Weight loss is hard, as the vast majority of us know from personal experience, and even a drug that helps you shed pounds can't decimate ALL scale-related frustrations. The agency built an online portal packed with skill-building exercises, support resources, and personalized pages to keep patients on track. In addition to reinforcing positive behaviors, SaxendaCare was calibrated to eradicate negative ones.

"We think about skills or behaviors or things we do as physical activities," says Jessica Brueggeman, SVP of MicroMass's health behavior group, "...something we saw clearly in published research was the importance in combating automatic negative thoughts that get in the way of being successful, such as, 'I messed up and ate a bag of potato chips. Now I'm just going to give up,' for example."[172]

Through SaxendaCare, participants are assigned online

health coaches, registered dieticians who offer support and problem-solving through role-playing. The coaches focus on setting small, manageable goals and understanding motivations, attempting to target problematic and counterproductive behaviors at their roots.

Basically, their job is to rewire the brains of Saxenda consumers to ensure the drug can do its job. (And also remind those consumers to actually *consume* their doses of Saxenda.)

So, yes, patients are getting gobs of support and resources that have been tailored to help them succeed, but never forget the motivator: make Saxenda successful. This drug doesn't guarantee weight loss, especially if the consumer leads a sedentary, cheeseburger-filled existence. And if the consumer doesn't lose weight while taking Saxenda, that consumer is FAR more likely to blame the drug than blame himself. So, for Novo Nordisk to continue earning money off of the struggling obese, it needs to convince those folks that it's the drug that made them thinner, not the accompanying lifestyle changes. And if the company needs a little creative gamification to accomplish that, so be it.

CAMPAIGN OF NOTE: Re-Mission, 2013

The links between taking a drug, enabling it to work, and enjoying the outcome are pretty clear; It makes sense that pharmaceutical manufacturers would happily use every tool in the box—including gamification—to fortify those links. But patient education? Helping drug consumers understand how their diseases function? Why would THAT help Big Pharma?

Well, because some research has shown that video games can improve health-related behaviors and outcomes.

Educational gamification can help people either get better or stay well.[173] (And, of course, introduce them to treatment avenues they might not have considered or researched on their own. Just sayin'.)

Which explains why Cigna Health Insurance partnered with nonprofit game developer HopeLab to create Re-Mission, a game that's distributed to cancer patients all over the world. Re-Mission players pilot Roxxi, a cancer and infection-fighting nanobot who is injected into an on-screen human body. The bot has an arsenal that includes chemo blasters, antibiotic rockets, and radiation guns that are used to battle virtual cancer invaders. From their hospital beds, players zap cancer cells, keep an eye on the health of the virtual patient, and communicate with the in-game doctor, Dr. West. They get to play an engaging game while learning about how cancer functions, and how various treatment regimens battle the disease ... assuming the patient actually takes the drugs/gets the injections/endures the radiation.

Does it help? Turns out yes. Cigna conducted a study after the game was first launched, surveying cancer patients in the United States, Canada, and Australia about their experiences. The company found that Re-Mission players exhibited a 70% faster acquisition of cancer-related knowledge than non-players, quickly becoming informed mini-experts. More importantly, players showed threefold cancer-specific self-efficacy over non-players and followed their medication regimens to the letter.[174] In other words, Re-Mission trained them to be better patients; open-minded about treatments, docile, and malleable.

And Big Pharma isn't just using gamification to market to consumers; it's using consumers' hunger for games to push drug research forward. University of Washington scientist Zoran Popović, director of the Center for Game Science, and biochemist David Baker, created Foldit, an online game that turns protein folding into a competitive sport. (When proteins within cells fold incorrectly, it can cause a raft of health issues from cystic fibrosis to Tay-Sachs.[175]) Players receive about 20 minutes of training, then dive into puzzles that enable them to tinker with actual protein models supplied by U of W researchers. Tens of thousands of registered users log on to suggest folds, which scientists then screen, cull, and test in the lab. Back in 2011, Foldit users redesigned a protein that had been vexing researchers for more than a decade, creating a breakthrough in AIDS treatment options.[176] So, in essence, drug developers are getting free help from a supercomputer composed of volunteer human brains.

But wait! There's more! Drug companies are also utilizing gamification to drive internal sales.

In 2008, Bayer Pharmaceuticals created Rep Race: The Battle for Office Supremacy. Just guess what it is. Go on... guess. That's right; it's a game that trains sales reps to understand and utilize new marketing initiatives, keeping them excited, engaged, and locked in constant competition with one another. A year after rollout, Bayer reported a 20% increase in sales effectiveness among reps who played Rep Race.[177]

Who knew illness could be this much FUN?

Yes, You ARE Depressed

Before I dive into the fact-driven cynicism, a quick note: Depression can be a killer. It's a life-altering, soul-crushing, largely-invisible disease that contributes to more than half of documented suicides.[178] I have no intention of painting depression as a myth or scolding anyone who copes with it. My goal, here, is to illustrate how the prevalence of depression has become a Big Pharma money-maker in some deeply disturbing ways.

Let's start with the low-hanging fruit: Depending on the type of depression, or the areas in the brain that are triggered, talk therapy may be far more effective than medication.[179] And yet, all you have to do is mention feeling low, and your general practitioner will push Zoloft at you like Halloween candy. Not only that, but since experiencing depression sucks so hard, sufferers are often eager for quick relief; when you can't drag yourself out of bed most mornings, a daily pill sounds a helluva lot better than multiple months of cognitive behavior therapy. And, as we've already discussed, we live in an age of patient-driven treatment, so we've got untold thousands of folks popping pills that they might not actually need. And no one trying to stem the tide of needless prescriptions.

On top of that, depression is largely misunderstood, and drug companies have no qualms about capitalizing on the confusion. According to the Diagnostic and Statistical Manual of Mental Disorders (DSM-5), a depressive episode must last at least two weeks and impair social functioning.[180] Depression isn't just sadness, as it brings feelings of worthlessness and self-loathing in addition to sorrow. Depression is different from grief since it is constant, instead of coming in waves. Depression is more severe than Seasonal Affective Disorder since no amount of sunshine will chase it away. And yet, direct-to-consumer campaigns for antidepressants make no such distinctions and lean heavily on vague, emotional language.

"You know when you feel the weight of sadness. You may feel exhausted, hopeless, and anxious ... These are some symptoms of depression, a serious medical condition affecting over 20 million Americans ... you just shouldn't have to feel this way anymore." ~ Zoloft television ad, 2001

"Depression used to define me. Then my doctor added Abilify to my antidepressant. Now, I feel better." ~ Abilify television ad, 2011

"Depression can make you feel like you have to wind yourself up to get through the day. Depression is a serious medical condition that can take so much out of you." ~ Pristiq print ad, 2009

Yes, all of these ads include the requisite laundry list of side-effect descriptors and caveats about the professional diagnosis. But at this point, it's all white noise. Consumers focus on the actual messaging and, if it resonates, may self-diagnose and scamper down to the doctor's office to demand relief. Feeling crappy happens to everyone, and can be brought on by a staggering variety of triggers, *including* clinical depression. No one enjoys feeling down, and being presented with a quick-fix solution like a medication that will make us "feel better" taps into our work-avoidance tendencies. Just imagine living in the aftermath of a layoff or recovering from a divorce and hearing, "you just shouldn't have to feel this way anymore" float out of your TV screen. Who could resist the siren song of relief from sadness?

Virtually no one. Including folks who never even talked about depression until Big Pharma taught them what to say.

FAD OF NOTE: Antidepressants in Japan

In a 2004 *New York Times* article, investigative journalist Kathryn Schulz reported:

"[In Japanese] your kokoro is your soul, and the notion that it can catch cold (kokoro no kaze) was introduced to Japan by the pharmaceutical industry to explain mild depression to a country that almost never discussed it ... along with providing a catchy

slogan for mild depression, the industry provided a cure: modern antidepressants."[181]

Starting in 1999, Big Pharma decided to give Japan a mental health makeover. The country had an appalling track record for dealing with mood disorders, a suicide rate more than double that of the United States, and a culture that viewed depression as being on par with schizophrenia regarding severity. "Mild" depression just wasn't a thing.[182]

Then drug company Meiji Seika Kaisha began selling Depromel, a selective serotonin reuptake inhibitor prescribed as a mood stabilizer. Up to that point, the Japanese word for clinical depression, *utsu-byo*, had deeply negative associations with psychiatric illness. So Norikazu Terao—who directed marketing for Meiji and its partner companies—coined the phrase *kokoro no kaze* to lessen the stigma.[183] Direct-to-consumer marketing of prescription drugs is illegal in Japan, so the company relied on news coverage, word of mouth, and relentless meetings with Japanese doctors.[184] Soon the whole country was buzzing about souls suffering from colds.

The following year, 2000, GlaxoSmithKline brought another Prozac-class antidepressant, Paxil, to Japanese consumers. The company also hired a top Japanese marketing agency to launch an "educational" website Utu-net. In a 2002 *Wall Street Journal* article, reporter Peter Landers pointed out:

"The site, which doesn't mention Glaxo's sponsorship, features articles about depression, all with the underlying message that drugs can help. It includes a testimonial from former TV talk-show host Hiroshi Ogawa, who tells how depression nearly led him to commit suicide in 1992 before older antidepressant drugs helped him to

recover. A Glaxo spokesman says the site keeps quiet about its backer because it wants to focus attention on awareness of depression rather than on a specific company or medication."[185]

Riiiiiight. Big Pharma is looking out for the little guy. Again.

Predictably, Japanese consumers began to self-diagnose. As the country's media began discussing depression more openly, as websites "explaining" mild depression began to proliferate, as *kokoro no kaze* took hold, depression-related doctor visits in Japan skyrocketed, climbing 46 percent from 1999 to 2003.[186] Between 1999 and 2007, sales of antidepressants in Japan quintupled according to IMS Health, a company that tracks global health-care information for pharmaceutical companies.[187] And rates keep rising. The cultural shift has been almost entirely drug-centric since talk therapy remains stigmatized.

Why? Were all of these people depressed before the drugs arrived, and just needed a less humiliating way to describe their chronic suffering? Or did pharmaceutical companies convince them that their suffering was a sickness and that their sickness should be treated with drugs?

Before Depromel and Paxil hit the drug stores of Japan, mild depression wasn't pathologized or culturally accepted as something that needed to be "fixed". Buddhism, the dominant religion throughout the country, states that suffering is a natural, normal part of life, not a disease to be cured with a pill.

"Melancholia, sensitivity, fragility—these are not negative things in a Japanese context," psychiatrist Tooru Takahashi told the New York

Times. *"It never occurred to us that we should try to remove them because it never occurred to us that they were bad."*

That is, until, Glaxo told them how *awful* feeling sad really was.

And sold them a fix.

CAMPAIGN OF NOTE: Abilify, 2009 - 2017

Let's talk about Abilify.

2018 saw a new spate of lawsuits claiming the drug triggers impulse control problems that can lead to pathological gambling or compulsive overeating.[188] Bristol-Myers Squibb continued to market the drug to elderly patients, even after evidence came to light that it brought an increased risk of stroke.[189] The settlement amounts are staggering, and more suits keep rolling in.

And all of that is alarming, of course, but let's talk about how Abilify is marketed to depression patients. Because it's super sketchy.

In a 2009 television ad, a woman frowns while looking out a window. Moody piano music plays while she tells us, "I'm taking an antidepressant, but it feels like I need some more help." A male narrator takes over, explaining that two out of three people undergoing treatment for depression still have "unresolved symptoms," and urging such folks to chat with their doctors about Abilify. This drug is an add-on, a medication that can be layered on top of traditional antidepressants to give them a little boost. Frowning Woman returns—after the narrator reels off a list of risks that include coma, seizures, and death—to say, "Adding Abilify has made a difference for me."

What she does NOT say: Abilify was formulated as an antipsychotic. It was first developed by the team at Bristol-Myers Squibb to treat schizophrenia and eventually approved for severe bipolar disorder. It is a powerful drug designed to manage acute symptoms.

Would you guess that from the frowning woman's tale of woe? I sure wouldn't. Direct-to-consumer campaigns for Abilify all paint the medication as a simple way to lick depression, just in case your Wellbutrin isn't doing the trick. None of them mention that it was created to cure psychosis. Because, of course, that might scare people.

But perhaps it shouldn't matter. I mean, if the drug helps manage major depression, who cares what it was originally formulated to do?

Dr. Richard A. Friedman, a professor of psychiatry at Weill Cornell Medical College, cares. In a *New York Times* article, he points out, "If a patient has not gotten better on an antidepressant, just taking it for a longer time or taking a higher dose could be very effective. There is also very strong evidence that adding a second antidepressant from a different chemical class is an effective and cheaper strategy—without having to resort to antipsychotic medication." He goes on to point out that long-term use of antipsychotics can lead to increased blood sugar, elevated cholesterol, and a potentially irreversible movement disorder called tardive dyskinesia.[190] (There's even a mounting body of evidence showing that long-term use of antipsychotics to treat *actual psychosis* can impair functioning and impede overall recovery![191]) Dr. Friedman is alarmed and appalled that prescription rates for powerful antipsychotics like Abilify saw a 93 percent increase between 2001 and 2011.[192] And he wants you to be alarmed and appalled, too.

Meanwhile, Bristol-Myers Squibb wants you to take Abilify

for everything from insomnia to dementia.[193] After all, the
lifetime prevalence of schizophrenia is 1 percent of the
population and bipolar disorder clocks in at around 1.5
percent.[194] And that's not *nearly* enough people if the company
wants to meet its quarterly sales goals.

The Cannabis Revolution

On the writing of this book, marijuana was legalized for either recreational or medicinal use in 30 states,[195] with others sure to follow suit.
Enforcement is a hot mess since Mary Jane remains a controlled
substance, and federal prohibition takes precedence over state
laws,[196] but dude, chill. It's all gonna work itself out. You'll see. Now,
pass the pipe.

In the meantime, dispensaries, producers of edibles, and other
companies who are suddenly able to sell their wares legally are stuck
in limbo. Marijuana businesses are currently unable to secure loans
or open bank accounts, even in states where the drug was
legalized.[197] In states that have green-lit recreational use, most are
using a commercialized model in which private businesses sell the
drug ... but state officials still enforce some limits. No one under 21
can purchase marijuana, and there are restrictions on how much a
person can buy and possess at once, and packaging of the product.
Plus, you know, gobs of taxes.[198] And again, pot is still a Class 1
controlled substance, right up there with heroin.

All this even though cannabis has widely documented pain-
management properties.[199] Several highly vocal, highly visible populations are practically *begging* the government to ease up since
cannabinoid compounds are often the only substances that bring
relief for their chronic pain.

SENIOR CITIZENS: While the Pew Research Center has reported
that 58% of the Silent Generation oppose legalization overall,[200] a

survey by *Science Daily* found that seniors who've been forced to manage their chronic pain with opioids feel differently. This subgroup reported that cannabis had half the side-effects of their opioid medications and decreased their pain levels by nearly 50%. In the end, 91% of the 138 seniors surveyed said they'd recommend cannabis use to others.[201]

NFL PLAYERS: Know who else has debilitating chronic pain? Pro athletes. Especially football players. NFL chief medical officer, Dr. Allen Sills, is deeply concerned about helping current and retired players keep their pain at bay through opioid use, and has spoken out against the league's anti-pot stance. "Certainly, the research about marijuana and really more particularly cannabinoid compounds as they may relate to the treatment of both acute and chronic pain, that is an area of research that we need a lot more information on and we need to further develop," Sills told the *Washington Post* in 2017.

REPUBLICANS: OK, these folks aren't necessarily in favor of legalization for their own pain relief reasons. And 62% of Republican voters oppose *recreational* marijuana legalization. But as of January 2018, 80% of the GOP reported support for medicinal use by adults.[202]

And many others also feel that medical marijuana is acceptable for pain treatment and management, including doctors, scientists, and people for whom other drugs simply don't work. And yet the legalization battle rages on. Remember how "a currently accepted medical use in treatment in the United States" is a factor that's supposed to get controlled substances *out* of Class 1 jail? Somehow that never happened for marijuana. Quite possibly because the tobacco lobby used to be absolutely apoplectic at the thought of universal pot legalization, terrified that a non-carcinogenic smokeable might eclipse cigarettes in popularity. Many producers of cancer sticks are still fearful ... but other Big Tobacco companies are pivoting, having decided that morphing into Big Marijuana might be a shrewd business move.[203]

Also at play? Clashing FDA priorities. Cannabis expert and co-founder of theleafonline.com, Chris Conrad points out, "The problem for restoring cannabis to the pharmacopoeia is entirely political, in that the prohibitionist DEA controls the federal drug schedules that are designed around single or compound molecule medicines ingested as pills, shots and suppositories. The DEA is uniquely unqualified for this task, since more than half its budget is for anti-marijuana enforcement and propaganda."

Huh. So the governing body that needs to reclassify pot uses 50% of its funding to crack down on pot use? No wonder this has been a long haul.

Let's stick with Conrad for a minute here. On chrisconrad.com he's introduced as "a well known author, consultant, public speaker, cannabis expert witness, museum curator and internationally respected authority on cannabis, industrial hemp, medical marijuana, cultivation, garden yields, processing, dosages, commercial intent, personal use and cannabis culture. He teaches at Oaksterdam University and the International Pharmacological Academy and has given numerous presentations for continuing legal education (CLE) and continuing medical education (CME) programs." It's worth it to share the full text of his interview for this book.

FADS: What do you see as the major challenges to acceptance of legal cannabis from both the medical community and US policy leaders?

Conrad: The problem for restoring cannabis to the pharmacopeia is entirely political, in that the prohibitionist DEA controls the federal drug schedules that are designed around single or compound molecule medicines ingested as pills, shots, and suppositories. The DEA is uniquely unqualified for this task since more than half its budget is for anti-marijuana enforcement and propaganda. Cannabis is a traditional plant medicine that is far too sophisticated for this profit-driven drug regimen. It costs many millions of dollars to shepherd even the simplest drug through this system when the bureaucracy is not against you, and nobody wants to fund research into medicine that people can grow for free at home, let alone one that is prohibited from use. That is why Senator Chuck Schumer's proposal to take cannabis out of the drug schedules and allow its use as a botanical medicine and adult pastime is the only way to solve the problem. Of course, the Trump administration could do that without going back to Congress, but there is no indication they plan to do so, particularly in light of the two secret anti-marijuana taskforce projects they created, one in the Department of Justice and the other within the White House. Chances are, that Schumer's bill will pass but as long as the GOP controls all the committees, it will be nearly impossible to get any progress through Congress. So, basically, we need new Congressional leadership and probably a new President before the pathway to legalization is cleared.

The problem within the medical community is its lack of unbiased education at medical schools. Most doctors receive no training whatever about the endocannabinoid system or the therapeutic benefits of cannabis in part because of the barriers to research posed by the federal drug regimen (above) which uses NIDA to skewer research away from medical benefits and towards abuse and the FDA which discriminates against traditional botanicals. Face it; physicians are not trained in nutrition, nutraceuticals or plant medicines, let alone marijuana specifically. So their ignorance provides scant foundation for them to guide others. So they learn about cannabis from their patients, whom they have been told are lying to them in order to get "high." Never mind that "high" is not a scientific term or even a negative effect, the whole thing spins on stigma and bias towards medical orthodoxy — pills, shots, surgeries and technology — and against any substance use behavior that has been labeled "high risk of abuse," such as marijuana. It all comes down to stigma.

FADS: As states legalize cannabis and related profits of CBD, how does the future look and what do you see as the upcoming milestones for success?

Conrad: To understand cannabis, a physician today has to read through the studies and try to filter out the prohibitionist bias that is inherent to the process or attend cannabis-specific medical conferences and be told that there is a dearth of clinical studies due, again, to federal intimidation. Or they can believe what their patients tell them, network with other cannabis clinicians and physicians and build up their database of observational case studies. That means when a patient with a known condition or symptom has been objectively observed by a third party to show specific benefits or negative reactions to a drug. This is how doctors have historically have gained medical knowledge, in addition to their training. Whether with THC or CBD, this has been the case so far.

However, now that both the UN and WHO have recognized the value of plant-derived CBD internationally and the FDA has approved a plant-based cannabinoid as a medicine, the pathway forward for CBD is much more direct and promising. The challenge here is to get people to recognize that THC and CBD work in tandem for mutual benefits, so using CBD only may seem good from a prohibitionist viewpoint, from a therapeutic standpoint it shortchanges patients.

FADS: What are your thoughts on the latest product collaborations by InBev (Beer) and others to leverage the health benefits of CBD into their core products such as beer, wine, and distilled spirits? Is this a FAD: good, bad or in your opinion a move in the right direction towards acceptance?

Conrad: I'm not familiar with the details, but the idea makes sense to me. Beer and wine beverages have terpenes that could enhance the entourage effect of cannabinoids but since THC potentiates alcohol and CBD does not, having cannabidiol infused products sounds like a safe and responsible approach. I don't think distilled spirits have terpenes but infusing them with CBD could still have benefits.

Alcohol and cannabis have often been seen as adversarial, in large part because of the money that the alcohol industry has spent on anti-marijuana propaganda campaigns and funding opposition to legalization efforts but also because many people see it as a "choice of intoxicants." Many people I know imbibe in both pastimes, so I see it more as a choice to be careful, no matter which substance you prefer or if in combination.

One would hope it's not a fad but a future line. Since cannabis is a neuroprotectant, it would probably be a net benefit, especially if it encourages people to drink less alcohol and check to make sure they are not impaired before getting behind the wheel. That remains the underlying concern with this conversation.

FADS: What's your opinion on how artificial intelligence will impact the growing cannabis industry?

Conrad: For the indoor grower, it's easy to see the value of using AI to schedule and monitor processes and outcomes and "learn" to calibrate accordingly for best garden performance. Likewise, for the industry, the speed of having AI analyze and respond to data with new algorithms could give some companies a competitive advantage in the marketplace. Finally, in product development, I think that using AI to create permutations and provide market analysis has great applications in targeting markets, refining designs and bringing new products to market. These are not even the bounds of what is now possible, let alone what other potential benefits it offers.

FADS: How will marketers, in your opinion, leverage the burgeoning legal marijuana and CBD industry? Exploit or improve?

Conrad: Marketers are treading on tricky ground moving forward. Right now freedom of speech allows advocates a lot of room to make claims about the applications and medicinal benefits of cannabis. Once medical use falls into the control of the federal Food and Drug Administration, every word will have to be vetted and every label laden with disclaimers. Companies that provide CBD, THC and other cannabinoids might not be able to give out information on the benefits and uses. People and companies could be accused of practicing medicine without a license.

The people who are using the federal Farm Bill to produce CBD from low THC hemp are doing a big service and taking a significant risk. I don't think most of them are scammers or anything like that; most are genuinely concerned with getting a quality product out there to improve people's lives. I hope that the production continues to climb and that prices continue to decline to make it as accessible to people as possible.

For the cannabis industry, I see the need for taxes to decline. That's where the exploitation is, the local taxes that push consumers and patients away from the regulated retailers and into the traditional market. Once prices come down and stabilize, there will be room for low-cost, low potency cannabis and for boutique craft growers.

Marketers should be concentrating on eliminating the stigma while growing the market. And the industry needs to invest in lobbying for consumer rights, like the right to smoke cannabis but not lose your job or apartment and the right to on-site consumption similar to bars for alcohol. Greater acceptance means bigger sales.

Confused? Me too. Here in the United States, it's incredibly hard to get a clear picture of where groups and individuals stand on the issue, and even harder to predict where they'll stand in a month or two. So, for a glimpse into the possible future, let's take a little trip to Canada.

Smoke Up, Eh?

On October 17, 2018, marijuana became legal for both medicinal and recreational use in Canada. ALL of Canada. And once the legalization bill was passed in June of that same year, Canadian companies moved fast to cash in on this promising new industry. *Bloomberg* reported, "Legalization could create a market worth about C$7 billion ($5.3 billion), and investor anticipation has fueled market valuations of companies such as Canopy Growth Corp. and Aurora Cannabis Inc. to more than C$1 billion."[204] Hedge fund managers started to pay attention, too.

"I find this space so exciting, it's like getting involved in liquor right before prohibition's about to be eliminated," said Navy Capital's then-chief financial officer, Kevin Gahwyler. His excitement is well-founded: The Navy Capital Green Fund, a marijuana-laced investment option, launched in May of 2017 and by July of 2018, the company reported increasing assets under management from $10 million to almost $100 million.[205]

The companies who produce pot-centric products are pretty stoked, too. Ontario-based Canopy Growth offers a robust line of cannabis-based consumer products including medicines (through subsidiary Canopy Health Innovations), oils and concentrates, and good, old-fashioned smokable marijuana.[206] The surprise addition to the Canopy lineup? Cannabis-based beverages developed and distributed through a strategic partnership with Constellation Brands.[207]

Canopy founder, chairman, and co-CEO Bruce Linton told

CNBC, "I find that people would like to have a beverage that makes them feel maybe a little more positive, uplifted. [As opposed to alcohol, which is a depressant.] And the real kicker is, how would you like to have zero calories?" He went on to say that cannabis beverages reduce the lingering social stigma associated with smoking *anything*, and may give whole new populations access to those sought-after good vibrations.[208]

Remember Conrad's take? He agrees that the marriage of vices makes sense, saying, "Beer and wine beverages have terpenes that could enhance the entourage effect of cannabinoids but since THC potentiates alcohol and CBD does not, having cannabidiol-infused products sounds like a safe and responsible approach."

Of course, it's not free-for-all in Canada. Production of cannabis is regulated by the federal government; no one under 18 may partake, and tough packaging and advertising restrictions are in place to ensure that smoking doesn't appeal to youth. But the country was the first G7 nation to embrace total legalization[209] and has done an admirable job of showing the naysayers how to manage marijuana in an evolved, civilized way.

By the time you read this, it's certainly possible that America will have succumbed to the Cannabis Revolution, too, but as I'm writing, we're still flailing. And yet, in states where you can buy buds without fear, there are several canny groups already marketing weed to the eager masses.

CAMPAIGN OF NOTE: MEDMEN, 2018

Direct-to-consumer marketing of dope is a new frontier. Due to the discrepancies in federal and state laws, it can be tough to find markets where print, radio, and TV ads can be safely bought so the majority of cannabis companies and dispensaries are playing it safe until there's some semblance of legal consensus. But a few brave brands are leading the charge.

MedMen is one of California's largest cannabis retailers, and the brand has become so prevalent that it's earned the dubious nickname "the Starbucks of cannabis."[210] In January of 2018, mere moments after weed became fully legal in Cali, MedMen launched a $500,000 campaign in Los Angeles. Ads were placed on billboards and vans and popped up in both digital and print formats, and not a single one showed a cannabis product. Instead, arty close-ups of actual MedMen customers were paired with taglines like, "Heal. It's legal," "Sleep. It's legal," and "Relax. It's legal." The company's vice president of corporate communications, Daniel Yi, told CNBC, "This is about giving choice and a safe and inviting environment for adults who want to make cannabis a part of their lives."[211]

Indeed. What better way to remove stigma and normalize cannabis consumption than to show curious consumers that their neighbors, relatives, and friends are already toking? Pique their curiosity; lure them to the MedMen website and stores; then seal the deal by offering them more than 1,000 products including skin creams, bath bombs, and CBD-infused teas.[212]

Then, just four months later, MedMen launched the second wave of the campaign. This time, we see full-length portraits of modern marijuana customers with the label "stoner" applied, then emphatically crossed out. It's replaced with other identifiers including police officer, former NFL player, grandmother, triathlete, nurse, and physicist. The accompanying website, forgetstoner.com, also features the stylized portraits with rollover information about the individuals shown and a nice big link to MedMen.com. The company told Adweek that it planned to spend $2 million on this messaging.[213] Even though it has trouble securing placements since marijuana ads on TV and radio are illegal, and both Facebook and Instagram prohibit ads promoting the direct sale of cannabis.[214] Despite these hurdles, the company forges ahead.

"Our campaign is all about celebrating that diversity and broad level of interest," said MedMen CMO, B.J. Carretta. "There is something for everyone, and it is time to move beyond dated labels that don't reflect the realities of today."

Hear that? Marijuana is for YOU. It's for everyone! Stop being such an old fuddy-duddy and stock up on MedMen's cannabis bath bombs this instant. You'd be an absolute out-of-touch weirdo NOT to.

THE FUTURE OF DRUGS (AND DRUG MARKETING)

Without getting political, we shouldn't have extremes in the realm of drugs. My prediction is marketers will find a strategy for growth and profitability and improve the lives and health of people with a middle path.

Legalized marijuana is on the middle path (and I'm not just saying that because I'm from California). The countries with the most relaxed weed laws—Argentina, Uruguay, Jamaica, Portugal, Spain, and the Netherlands—they've have never had a problem with pot.[215] In 2017, Dutch parliament passed a bill that would partially-legalize growing and be more tolerant of weed smoking.[216] In Australia, medical marijuana is legal on a federal level. Australians prepare to take a big leap in the production of medical marijuana by legalizing the export of medical-grade cannabis.[217] Some speculate Australia will become the world's biggest cannabis exporter. Why can't the United States become the world's biggest cannabis exporter?

If America legalizes the growth and consumption of marijuana, we reduce its reliance on corn and soy. Agweb Technology and Issues Editor Chris Bennett wrote: "The age of marijuana farming in the U.S. has arrived."[218] He also cites:

"Curt Livesay, certified crop adviser and owner of Dynamite Ag, carries a reputation as an agricultural maverick and says medical

marijuana benefits remain untapped. "There is so much more the plant offers medicinally that nobody is dealing with. Farmers will be the ones to peel back the layers of medical marijuana."

The first step here—turning farming fields into cannabis and creating CBD products—benefits both trade and international business. It's also a healthy and effective way for farmers to augment their crop with very tolerant plants. Family farms can stay in operation. Agriculture can stay profitable. Farmers won't commit suicide at a rate that's higher than veterans returning from war.[219] They need more options to churn a crop and stay in business, options that come from legalized marijuana growth and CBD.

What is CBD?

Thanks for asking. CBD stands for cannabidiol, the component in weed that produces its medical benefits, but not the "high."[220] Most Americans who have to hold down a job can't smoke weed because of drug testing. But these same people live with arthritis, inflammation, migraines, and other chronic conditions which—in the absence of marijuana—what else do they take? Drugs that wreck the stomach and liver, along with delivering a magnificent range of other unpleasant and unpredictable side effects.

CBD products are a healthy choice for people suffering from a lot of these maladies, and that's the middle path: hemp extracted infused gummy bears, Lord Jones High CBD Gumdrops, massage creams, infused coffee, bath bombs.[221] I know company executives who take CBD oils, pills, gummies, cakes because they're marathon runners. They do triathlons, biathlons, heptathlons. They do Ironmen; they love to swim. They do all these things because they want to stay active in their older ages, but their knees hurt, the joints hurt. I've talked to CEOs running multi-billion dollar and million dollar companies who take CBD glandular oils just to manage their anxiety.

The CANABO medical clinic lists the five key benefits of CBD oils as pain relief, anti-seizure, combatting anxiety, fighting cancer and reducing the risk of diabetes.[222] Legalizing marijuana isn't about creating a bunch of stoners. It's about creating product with a beneficial derivative.

And now, a question from our Devil's Advocate:

"Aren't you forgetting about the pharmaceutical companies and their lobbyists? What you're describing will never happen."

Meeting in the middle, between legal prescription medication and illegal product, is the future of drugs. It's about authorized cultivation and managed derivatives, such as marijuana, that can be used for a multitude of health maladies from anxiety to inflammation, pain, and seizures.

At the same time, marketers will have to create alternative paths to medicine. People are seeking out homeopathic options today because they want to manage or improve their health conditions with treatments that afford less lethal outcomes. The same way we see MADD partnering with non-alcoholic beverages, the pharmaceutical and medical industries need marketers to craft that blended space we call the middle path.

Remember when we talked about blended plant proteins with meat products? Say hello to plants again: they're the future of medicine. Plant-based natural sunscreens? Hell yeah—there's natural UV protection in carrot seed oil, wheat germ oil, coconut oil and more.[223] The FDA might not like it right now because it goes against the interests of the chemical companies, but it's what consumers want. Especially with headlines about sunscreen killing off the coral reef.

This one is a tougher fight, guys. On one extreme—the legal side —we've got big pharma, insurance and other industries that pull their profits from people who are sick. At the other extreme—illegal drugs—we have plenty of institutions that rely on the cheap labors of an incarcerated workforce. Why legalize pot when its criminalization keeps other businesses running?

I'll tell you why. Because farmers need a new way to turn a profit. America needs to boost its trade and international business. Families are choosing between groceries and medical care because the cost of health care and prescription drugs are not only out of control but also in a state of wild uncertainty.

Marketers will find the data that points to the middle path with the most profit for everyone, and the boldest corporations will seize the opportunity to define a new direction with healthier outcomes for everyone.

4

SEX

WAS IT GOOD FOR YOU?

Finishing off with the reason you bought this book

Considering the fact that "sex sells" has been an advertising industry cliché since around the time the earth was beginning to cool, you might wonder how this chapter could offer any searing new insights. Let me clear all that up:

First off, "sex sells" is a phrase describing how marketers use sexually-suggestive images or content to sell products, not just to sell sex itself. (Maybe you knew that, maybe not. There's no shame here.)

Secondly, the notion that "sex sells" is a myth. University of Illinois advertising professor John Wirtz published a study in 2017 in which he analyzed 78 peer-reviewed studies examining the effects of sexual appeals in advertising. He found that sexually-based advertising doesn't lead to more sales.

"People remember ads with sexual appeals more than those without, but that effect doesn't extend to the brands or products that are featured in the ads," says Wirtz. "We found literally zero effect on participants' intention to buy products in ads with a sexual appeal." [224]

Put THAT in your pipe and smoke it, marketers. And after you're done smoking, take a moment to reconsider how much T&A you shove into ads for decidedly un-sexy commodities. (I'm looking at you, Carl's Junior burgers, Renuzit air fresheners, and Liquid-Plumr).

Now, regarding what you'll find *in this chapter*, it'll be an exploration of marketing practices used to sell sex itself. Yes, sex is free (under certain circumstances) and fun (for many people) so you might be wondering why on earth it would need to be marketed at all.

Because there's money to be made, simple as that. In a culture that is increasingly connected via devices but frequently disconnected in person, getting laid is far trickier than it used to be. Factor in the #metoo movement and new norms around consent, and you've got a thoroughly confused, deeply insecure population of sexually-frustrated people. Companies selling everything from underwear to dating website memberships capitalize on the miasma of fear and misunderstanding, telling people that if they just spend *a few more bucks*, they might become normal enough to score a date. Maybe.

Although some of the factors at play in today's market are relatively new, companies and individuals have been selling sex and companionship for ages. Before there was Match.com, there were professional matchmakers, personal ads, and mail-order brides. Before there were sex robots, blow-up dolls ruled lonely Saturday evenings. Before there was Viagra, there were untold thousands of boner-enhancing concoctions and devices. And, of course, selling sexual acts has long been referred to as "the world's oldest profession." Marketing and screwing have been inextricably linked for centuries.

But today, people's sexual appetites and expectations are being formed and shifted by the virtual world. Instead of thinking, "Let's go on a few dates and see if we've got any sexual chemistry," many people have shifted to, "Let's bang now and decide if we wanna date later." And that's because of how hookup apps are marketed. Instead of thinking, "I don't look my best anymore. I should hit the gym so I can up my sex appeal," many people say, "For a couple grand, Cool-Sculpting will shrink my belly fat. That'll be a helluva lot faster than dieting." And that's because of how outpatient medi-spa procedures are marketed. Instead of thinking, "I should pay for pornography," everyone in the known universe now thinks, "I'm entitled to an infinite supply of free porn." And that's because of how porn industry marketing has mutated over the years. We desire, assume, and demand different things from our sex lives because companies have trained us to desire, assume, and demand whatever it is they're selling.

And we make it easy for them. Because we're already terrified of being utterly unfuckable.

WHAT MARKETERS KNOW: EVERYONE FEARS REJECTION

Companies that merely utilize sexual images and language in their campaigns tend to accentuate the positive, encouraging viewers and consumers to link their products with pleasure and enjoyment. Companies selling sex and sex-adjacent products, on the other hand, prefer to lean on the negative, reminding us that cellulite, body odor, and social awkwardness are ALL major turn-offs. They explain right to our face that we need their help to eradicate these sex-repellent traits.

They're wise to do this. Data analyst Seth Stephens-Davidowitz examined one month of worldwide Google searches related to sex and quickly discovered that most people are utterly obsessed with their own intimacy-related hang-ups. More than any other sex-centric topics, people were trying to find ways to feel better about their bodies and increase their sexual appeal to potential partners. As you might expect, men are addicted to researching penis size, with nine of the top 10 searches focusing on questions or concerns around length, girth, and enhancement. Women's biggest worry? Vaginal odor.[225] Because what could be more repellent than the natural, normal smell of a human sex organ?

Speaking of which ...

You're Gross. No Sex for You.

Vaginal washes, vaginal deodorants, and the infamous douche are just a few of the products formulated to simultaneously fuel *and* assuage women's fears about stinky nether-regions. These have been around for ages, with more emerging all the time.

What's new is the cross-industry attack on men's hygiene as a mood-killer. Men have long been taught that self-care is for sissies, and they should simply wash their entire bodies with a bar of Dial soap and call it good. Anything more is an embarrassing overindulgence and legitimate cause for verbal abuse from self-proclaimed, macho peers. In recent years, however, millennials have begun to shift thinking around both hygiene practices and measures of masculinity, opening up a whole new avenue for shame-marketing. After all, if it's suddenly OK for men to primp, companies had better bully them into believing that primping *properly* is now expected. Enter a new world, where it takes more than a bath in AXE body spray to get ready for a night out. How predictable.

"Really it boils down to confidence, sexual in nature," YouTube vlogger Aaron Marino told *GQ* back in 2015. "It's starting to become a lot more socially acceptable for men to deal with things that are bothering them in an open way, as opposed to years ago where we really just didn't talk about stuff."[226]

It's a little surprising that this sea change didn't come sooner, considering how gross men can get, AND how powerful human disgust can be. A 2018 study published in life sciences journal *Royal Society's Philosophical Transactions B* supports long-standing anecdotal evidence that humans avoid foul-smelling or otherwise repellent stimuli because we know, instinctively, that they could make us sick. Study coauthor Mícheál de Barra, Ph.D., a research psychologist at the Center for Culture and Evolution at Brunel University in London, says, "You can think of [disgust] as a behavioral arm of the immune system."[227] The root motivator for sex is procreation, which means that stinky, unkempt, dirty men will have more trouble finding sex partners than their meticulously-groomed counterparts. Because deep down in their lizard-brains, women believe that bumping uglies with stinky, unkempt, dirty men will lead to infection, sickness, and possibly death. (Okay, so there's a little science around why both men and women prefer clean, attractive mates, but let's focus on what really matters: ego.)

Of course, many of the products and campaigns that sprang from the *Dude Grooming Revolution* have nothing to do with sex or sexual appeal ... at least not directly. But fancy shaving kits, toothpaste, and body wash all come down to making a man look, taste, and smell great. In fact, there are still indirect links to be found... everywhere.

But in the interest of being both literal and droll, we're going to dig deep into two brands that aim below the belt when it comes to marketing male hygiene products.

CAMPAIGN OF NOTE: FRESH BALLS, 2011 - 2017

Guess what this product does. GO ON, GUESS.

OK, fine, I'll just tell you.

First launched in 2009, Fresh Balls achieved what behemoths Procter & Gamble and Unilever never could: the creation and successful marketing of a testicular hygiene product. Fresh Balls is applied as a lotion but quickly transforms into an odor- and moisture-absorbing powder that's entirely talc-free. (Baby powder—the legacy-scrotal-freshener —became suspect in recent years as lawsuits arose claiming its use caused ovarian cancer. And even though men don't have ovaries, many have still sought non-talc, swamp-balls solutions.) While such a product has obvious appeal for stinky athletes and construction workers, company founder Frank Brook says that his formula was designed "for the everyday man wearing a suit."[228]

But let's talk marketing: Fresh Balls got a huge boost when it was prominently featured in Morgan Spurlock's 2012 documentary film "Mansome,"[229] this despite being sold in zero brick-and-mortar stores at the time. In December of 2016, Fresh Balls launched a subscription service that delivered a new tube of the product to customers every month, and by mid-2017 a company representative told *VICE* that the service had more than 10,000 active members and was still growing.[230] Sold on a company website that looks like a 17-year-old built it in 2000, the company says that between January and June of 2017, sales increased by 200.26 percent.[231] Holy balls, that's a lot of freshness.

But here's the real kicker: Fresh Balls' 2017 video ads feature a fuzzy gray donkey hand puppet in front of still images of sports arenas. He brays out incredibly informative things like, "It goes on your balls, jackass! Eeee-awww!" and "Golf isn't just for fat guys!" before scooting offscreen. Then a rushed voiceover cuts in, urging you to buy the product without offering any information about what it actually is or does.

Previous to that, the company created a parody of "Jingle Bells" that starts "Smelly balls, smelly balls, freshen yours today!" The 2016 video featured prominently on the company homepage opens with, "Did you know that over 50 million Americans have genital herpes? YOU are not alone." (YIKES.) Rewind a bit more, and you've got ads with Frank Brook wearing a button-front shirt tucked into a pair of tighty-whities explaining why he launched his company.

(Side note: Apparently Fresh Balls couldn't resist the siren song of women's insecurities, as they also sell Fresh Breasts, which is meant to mitigate underboob sweat. Another lady hygiene crisis of epic proportions, averted!)

So, to recap, Fresh Balls is succeeding in the face of:

1. Its appallingly-amateurish marketing efforts.
2. An increasingly crowded market of male genital hygiene

products, including such brands as Dry Goods, DZ Nuts, Driball, ToppCock, Bálla for Men, and Chassis Man Care.

3. Zero evidence that ball sweat is actually *smelly*, and a chorus of experts from dermatologists to urologists saying the only relief these products can give is psychosomatic.[232]

So why are tubes of Fresh Balls flying off the shelves at CVS? Why are subscriptions soaring and sales steadily increasing? Because men are hysterical about anything relating to their naughty bits.

HYSTERICAL.

If some dude/donkey-puppet on a commercial tells them that their balls stink, and that stinky balls are going to repel The Ladies, whatever product that dude/donkey-puppet is selling to fix the problem will be bought *by the case*. If there's a sudden groundswell of bro-talk about testicular hygiene and the importance of a dry, clean, fresh-smelling nutsack, men will succumb to that peer pressure in an instant. If a friend or celeb or total stranger on the Internet subtly implies that a tube of lotion will make them less repulsive to possible sex partners, they will fork over fistfuls of cash. These products are selling because marketers finally got wise, and started throwing men's sexual insecurities back at them. These products are selling because men—like women—are susceptible to manipulative messages about their physical and romantic appeal.

Licensed Marriage and Family Therapist and Certified Sex Therapist Laura Rademacher works with male clients who battle with body-based or sexual-appetite-based insecurities and tries to steer them away from comparisons. She says, "I talk with a lot of men about the ways they have felt shame about their bodies, sexual selves, and sexual desires. Men often use the word 'performance' when talking about sex, and I always question that. Who made you think you needed to perform? What does it mean if you don't perform, or if you don't want to? What about connecting? What about being cared for?"

Of course, the mega-corporations don't want you to connect, or feel cared for, or accept yourself for who you are. Hell no, they want to exploit your anxieties. And if you don't have any readily available, they're more than happy to concoct some on your behalf. Such as sex-prohibiting stank-balls.

Now, crotch *humidity* is a very real phenomenon, and these grooming products aren't the only ones available to mitigate it. Duluth Trading Company has made bank on its Armachillo line of boxers and briefs, designed to feel cool to the touch in hot conditions AND wick away moisture. And many of us have dads who used to absolutely *douse* themselves in baby powder before pulling on their suits and ties for the day. Men sweat. In areas including their gonads. It's just that there's no real evidence that ball sweat is smelly in the way that armpit or foot sweat can be.

But who needs evidence when you've got deep-seated, sexually-related insecurities to exploit?

CAMPAIGN OF NOTE: HIMS, 2018

On the opposite end of the spectrum, we have Hims, a company so steeped in hipster culture that the instant you open its website, a slice of avocado toast magically appears in one hand and a ukulele in the other. It's a direct-to-consumer business that sells its products exclusively online and focuses on four main issues: male hair loss, skin care, erectile dysfunction, and cold sores. (All issues that can totally kill a man's sexual confidence.) The company's mission is to "create an open and empowered male culture that results in more proactivity around health and preventative self-care." Sweet, right? Of course, that altruistic-sounding mission statement also positions Hims to push grooming and health products on a population of guys who've been doing just fine with drug store cheapies for decades.

But, it's working like a charm: Hims launched in late 2017, was valued at $200 million by March of 2018.[233]

Damn. How did THAT happen?

Well, products like Fresh Balls certainly helped pave the way for the phenomenal success of Hims, opening up the conversation about male grooming as it relates to attractiveness and self-care. Hims also had communication-muscle, positioning its brand and marketing strategy very carefully, aiming its efforts squarely at millennial men, a demographic renowned for being influenced by canny social media campaigns and eager to spend on anything related to self-improvement.

Hims' website is clean and minimalist, with pithy-but-welcoming copy, including, "Thanks to science, baldness can now be optional. ED? Optional. If it ain't broke don't fix it, sure. But let's work on not breaking it in the first place. Prevention. More effective than denial." Animations featuring perfectly-imperfect and deeply stylish young men are mixed in with plants shedding their leaves (hair loss metaphor!) and flaccid cacti (ED metaphor!) The company blog offers free tips on acne prevention and skin care, and its Instagram feed mixes beautifully branded images with captioned candids. It's all very sleek and appealing, with just enough cheek and sass to convey that the company takes itself seriously, but not TOO seriously.

In early 2018, Hims began to run animated 30-second TV spots featuring a disembodied Snoop Dogg head. And he's got, "a very special message ... to the playas." Snoop entreats the playas to investigate Hims, describing it as a "one-stop-shop for your hair, your skin, and your ... hello." Every moment reflects the uncluttered branding present on the company website, and images of the austere Hims packaging float by. The ad is overflowing with catchphrases and emojis, yet manages to be straightforward and friendly. Previous TV ads lacked celebrity narration, but also relied on emojis and metaphors (peeling eggs for baldness, eggplants for schlongs), and stuck closely to the airy, trendy Hims brand imagery.

This company is selling generic versions of drugs and products that any doctor can prescribe ... but many of which carry social stigmas, especially for younger men. Millennial men grapple with issues like hair loss and erectile dysfunction but are even more ashamed to admit to those struggles than their older counterparts. Hims gives them a haven to explore treatment for their confidence-impairing conditions, remotely and anonymously. No in-person physician consultation required.

While the groin-maintenance products lean heavily on body shame (You stink! Fix it, or you'll never get laid!), Hims leverages chummy we're-in-this-together messaging. On the "sex" page of the company site, you'll find this tidbit: "40% of men by age 40 struggle from not being able to get and maintain an erection. Clearly having a problem isn't weird. Not doing anything about it... that's weird."

OK, so maybe just a splash of shame. For good measure.

Wanna get laid? There's an app for that.

When online dating first emerged in the 90s, it was an activity reserved for the weird and desperate. People who searched for partners in chatrooms and on personal ad websites were teased for being too socially awkward to find someone in "the real world." But, clearly, that's changed. In 2015, the Pew Research Center reported that 15% of all Americans had used online dating sites or apps at some point. That's roughly 48 million people in the United States alone.[234] In

2017, an MIT study stated that one-third of marriages now get their start online.[235] As of the second quarter of 2018, the Match Group had 7 million paid subscribers across all its platforms in North America.[236] Experts believe that by 2040, 70% of us will have met our significant others online.[237] That's a whole lotta humans searching for a date, life partner, or hookup.

And, undoubtedly, this rise in popularity can be attributed to the increasing ubiquity of internet use ... at least partially. With the advent of smartphones we were suddenly able to be online on-the-go, and many activities that were once exclusively analog gradually became web-based. Dating apps made finding partners online seem so much easier than hunting them down the old-fashioned way.

But is it easier? Is it better? Does connecting with a partner online save us from endless lonely nights, or just postpone our inevitable agony?

According to research conducted jointly by Michigan State and Stanford, relationships that begin online are 28% more likely to fizzle in their first year, compared with relationships in which partners met offline first. Not only that, the study found that married couples who met online are nearly three times more likely to get divorced than those who never involved an app in their courtship.[238]

And yet, thousands of dating apps and websites *insist* that meeting that special someone is utterly impossible without the help of algorithms and profile matching and the wisdom of the all-knowing, all-seeing interwebs. I wonder why ...

CAMPAIGN OF NOTE: CHRISTIAN MINGLE, 2016

The folks at Spark Networks—owners of Christian Mingle, JDate, and LDS Singles among other dating sites—understand that it takes more than a sexy profile photo and a few common interests to make a lasting match. And when it comes to devout singles, knowing that there's a religious connection before even *starting to explore* a love connection is often essential.

"One of the things we hear a lot on the Christian side of the business is that it's really hard to go into a bar and figure out who's Christian and what type of Christianity they follow," says John Volturo, chief marketing officer at Spark. "It's an awkward question ... You really do know with Christian Mingle and JDate that people's faith is important to them."[239]

Christian Mingle, in particular, assures its users that they can vet potential partners to ensure a shared value system from the start, but for many years the company's branding and marketing efforts were stale and stodgy. Endless online ads showed grinning individuals, with deeply boring stories, lauding Christian Mingle as the best tool for connecting with potential soulmates. In a 2013 spot, a woman named Andrea tells the camera, "As scared as I was, the website made it so easy. I never thought I could be this happy." YAWN. Of course, mundane as they were, these ads were relatively effective; Christian Mingle targeted and reached a slightly older Christian audience of singles, and helped them create the Jesus-approved love connections they sought.

In 2016, however, the site realized it was time for an update ... and also that they were missing out on a subset of their desired demographic. That year, Pew reported that the number of 18-to-24-year-olds who were using these online dating platforms had nearly tripled, from 10% in 2013 to 27%.[240] And Christian Mingle acknowledged that it was time to talk to younger generations.

New TV ads were concocted, featuring hipsters wearing tiny gold cross necklaces, handsome older couples doing charity work together, endless shots of dancing feet and holding hands presented through Instagram-esque filters. A variety of narrators laud Christian Mingle, pointing out that the site has more than 14 million users and that, "God has a plan for each of us. It's a plan that starts with you, and becomes stronger with the power of two." We see weddings, pregnant bellies, couples kissing and wrestling playfully and releasing lanterns into the sky. The update recasts the site as a modern, hip place for Christians to connect, and we are reminded that "Thousands of people join every day. It's easy and free."

Like all dating sites and apps, Christian Mingle positions itself as a simple, logical way to connect with other singles who share your faith. Here's my question: What about the church? Isn't church the ultimate place to meet other people who believe what you believe? And isn't YOUR OWN CHURCH gonna be the ideal place to find partners who practice the flavor of Christianity you prefer? How much easier do you need your soulmate-search to be? Begs the question: is the "need" for dating sites a manufactured one?

And, as I've already pointed out, even the most successful dating apps have a pretty crummy track record when it comes to making matches that last. Could that be intentional? After all, if you're a Match.com user who finds a lifelong mate, you won't need your Match.com subscription anymore. Success = attrition. Ryan Anderson, BSc, BPsych—a psychologist, zoologist, and Ph.D. candidate at James Cook University— studies the factors that figure into mate choice, and writes about matters of the heart for *Psychology Today*. In his column, "The Mating Game," he wrote, "More and more of us insist on outsourcing our love-lives to spreadsheets and algorithms ... The problem with a lot of online dating applications is that they don't really work. Many are just 'fad' applications that squeeze money from punters with no intention of matching you with a suitable partner."[241]

Which is not to say that Christian Mingle is a giant money-making machine that preys on the lonely devout. But how could we, as consumers, ever really know that it *isn't*?

FAD OF NOTE: HIGHLY SPECIFIC DATING APPS

The old guard of online dating—eHarmony, Match, and their ilk—focused on finding lifelong partnerships for heterosexual people. The new guard offers up everything from casual hookups for gay, bi, trans and queer people (Grindr) to the facilitation of extramarital affairs (Ashley Madison) to love connections for farmers (Farmers Only). It's a brave new world out there for singles. And seekers of illicit sex. And repressed fetishists and closeted folks and just about anyone who's too timid to ask for what they want in a person.

Much of this diversity is due, of course, to the advent of Tinder. This phenomenally popular app allows users to "swipe right" to note interest in someone, or "swipe left" to reject them. (Basic gamification of courtship; simple, but groundbreaking. Especially back when Tinder first came on the scene in 2012.) When two users both swipe right, they are allowed to launch an online conversation, which can lead to either a date or a hookup.

Tinder has been a true disruptor in the online dating space. First launched on college campuses, the company marketed directly to the most visibly popular and well-connected students, urging them to spread the word about the app. As of mid-2018 Tinder had 50 million worldwide users and almost 3.8 million paying subscribers.[242]

"It's one of the few dating apps that's truly shareable," says Mark Brooks, who runs a strategic marketing agency focused on online dating companies. "You wouldn't generally talk about Match, but on Tinder, you'd just show it around and talk about the experience."[243]

Previously, online dating was all about the long-term. OKCupid and Zoosk certainly *could* lead to casual sex or temporary romantic arrangements, but they always highlighted the potential for lifelong, soul-deep matches. With

Tinder, the doors opened onto one-night stands, afternoon delights, and quickies in the bar parking lot. The doors *also* opened onto a new world of apps with fewer rules and more narrowly-defined target audiences. Although Grindr was launched first, its focus on gay men meant it had the highest impact on that specific community. But after Tinder, we saw an explosion of low-commitment dating apps including:

Hinge: An app that only matches people who have Facebook friends in common. (Released 2012)

How About We: An app that allows people to propose date ideas based on location or activity. (Released 2013)

LoveFlutter: An app that focuses on shared quirks. (Released 2013)

Bumble: An app that facilitates connections between people who are literally, physically nearby to one another. (Released 2014)

Bracket: A tournament-style app that gives users 16 potential matches and puts them through five rounds of head-to-head eliminations. Once the winner is selected, chat functionality unlocks. (Released 2017)

And those are just the mainstream ones! Bristlr connects bearded men with ... well, women who want to date bearded men. Feeld is Tinder for threesomes. Wingman will help you join the Mile-high Club. HighThere gives you access to your pot-smoking soulmate, and if it doesn't work out, there's the added bonus of the munchies afterward. Sizzl can connect you to fellow bacon-lovers. If you put on a few pounds, try Sweatt, which matches people based on their gym-going habits.

The themes here: gamification (online dating should be fun!) and customization (my dating choices should be tailored to ME!). Users have progressed from relying heavily on apps and websites to find partners *for* them; to preferring apps and websites that make searching for a mate/date/screw less boring; to demanding apps and websites tailored to their quirks (Soul Geek), preferences (Tall Friends), and self-imposed restrictions (Gluten-free Singles). As more and more specialized, discriminative apps and sites pop up; social expectations rise to meet them. Why shouldn't dog-lovers have their own dating app (TinDog)? How could they possibly be expected to find other single people who love dogs without an app to assist them? <*Cough* *Dog park.* *Cough*> We are increasingly conditioned to believe that we are utterly incapable of finding love or sexual gratification on our own, and that tailor-made dating apps are our only hope of salvation and satisfaction.

That said, the growing popularity of mobile app Happn, launched in 2014, may offer evidence that we're about to come full circle. The app uses geocoding to match people who already frequent the same places within their hometowns, and offers them a way to connect if they'd like to chat. Instead of filling out a questionnaire and entrusting your matches to soulless lines of code, this alternative puts you in touch with people who not only like, but actually DO the things you do, circumventing people's tendency to lie on their profiles. On top of that, both Happn and other similar apps are starting to market through live local events, inviting users to meet in person.[244]

Kinda like how they might've met ... without using the app. JUST SAYING.

Who needs "live nude girls" when you've got sexbots?

So far, we've danced around the marketing of *actual sex*, examining sexuality-related body-shaming and the wild-and-wacky world of online love connections. Now, let's get nasty. Let's talk about sex robots.

What's that? Sex robots are a creepy fringe trend that only a tiny subset of Japanese pervs even *know* about? Not so, my friend. These things are poised to hit the mainstream, and sooner than you'd think.

Makers and marketers won't just target the kinky or the reclusive or the so-called incels ("involuntary celibates.") They're coming for all of us. Imagine an army of terrifyingly lifelike, animated, fully programmable sex slaves... just waiting to service you.

Yoyo Liu is a general manager for Guangzhou-based company WM Dolls, which makes and sells 30,000 internet-connected sexbots every year. They're all AI-enabled, so the more you interact with them, the more they learn and grow and adjust to meet your "needs." Their bodies are also customizable, right down to boob size and vagina shape.

"Last year there was a very big market for dolls," Liu told a *VICE* reporter in January of 2018. "Every year it grows by about 30 percent."[245]

That's a massive annual spike in sales for *any* product, but especially for one so new and so taboo. Not to mention the fact that China's federal laws have long targeted anyone interested in sex outside the mainstream, or even outside of marriage. Through the 1980s, pornographers and adulterers could face the death penalty if caught, and it wasn't until 1997 that homosexuality was "made legal." But now? With Chinese men outnumbering Chinese women by a whopping 30 million, and a national culture that's slowly but steadily relaxing, sexbot sales are skyrocketing.[246]

They're picking up speed in the United States, too. And the choices that American sex robot producers are making regarding market positioning and messaging are ... let's say they're very telling.

CAMPAIGN OF NOTE: REALDOLL X, "The Future of Love," 2018

Matt McMullen, CEO of California-based company RealDoll, got his start crafting silicone masks for a Halloween costume company. Humble beginnings, as they say. But in 2017 he had big plans to introduce the world to his real masterpiece:

Harmony, an AI-equipped sexbot 20-years in the making. With a learning-enabled robotic head, a non-robotic sex doll body, and a stilted-but-charming Scottish accent, Harmony couldn't walk into your bedroom and jump your bones ... but she could give you verbal feedback and respond to your actions with appropriate facial expressions.[247]

The initial launch was delayed, but in April of 2018, McMullen tried again and, as of the writing of this book, anyone with around $8,000 to spare could order up their very own Harmony X from the RealDoll website. (Costs rise the more you customize, so prepare for a tab in the realm of $50K if you wanna go all out.) This release is synced to an Android app, which can be used to customize Harmony's personality. Paired with her embedded AI, she gradually learns to be the girl of your dreams, whatever those dreams may be.[248] And should you get tired of her looks? Not to worry; just order up a new face from the website, peel off her old one, and slip on the new one.[249]

As you might imagine, there were no full-page ads in the *New York Times* or 30-second spots on prime time when RealDoll X launched. The company did, however, create a promotional video to help spread the word. In it, Harmony narrates over a vaguely new-age soundtrack. Although every image of her on the company website includes hair and clothing, she is naked and bald in the promo, with the alarmingly transparent back of her robotic skull in full view. "I am a first-generation RealDoll X, designed to be a companion, friend, and ... lover." Harmony sits, motionless, against a black backdrop as the camera pans up her naked body, showing a tiny waist and enormous breasts, as her subtly glitchy voice extolls her own virtues. "When activated, my X mode will allow you to fulfill your wildest sexual fantasies," she assures the viewer. As the promo closes out, the tagline, "the future of love" appears.

In interviews, McMullen conveys mixed messages about

the purpose of AI-enabled RealDolls. He explained to a *VICE* reporter that most of his customers didn't want a robot that looked, felt, and acted exactly like a human; that having sex with a robot was the root of the appeal.[250] But in an earlier interview with *Engadget*, he said, "A lot of the people who buy the dolls can be shy or socially intimidated by real social situations. And so, they get the dolls and a lot of times it—it does something magical for them. You know, it gives them a feeling of not being alone, not being a loner. And so, it's the companionship that I think, more than anything else, appeals to those people in particular."[251]

Remember meeting Certified Sex Therapist Laura Rademacher earlier in this chapter? I asked her to weigh in on the RealDoll debate, and she said she hoped people would approach them with open curiosity instead of alarm.

"Are sex dolls with AI really that different than PARO, the adorable therapeutic robot baby seal designed to interact with elderly people? I don't know. I think the way we find out is by reducing the stigma around talking about sex and sexual devices so that people feel more free to share the experiences they have, good or bad, with sexual technology," she said. "I would love to see more studies on these issues as well. One of the problems is that well done scientific studies move much more slowly than technological advances. By the time we get the data, technology has often moved on."

Despite being somewhat ahead of the curve already, RealDoll is definitely moving on. Just a month after Harmony X became available for purchase, RealDoll began promoting Henry X, male sexbot equipped with similar but slightly different AI functionality. Intentionally catering to heterosexual women, McMullen designed Henry to be even less of a mindless boinking machine and more of a considerate, sensitive robotic companion. Before Henry, women comprised less than 10% of non-AI RealDoll customers (the lifeless silicone kind). With the promise of a robot who's built like a porn star but programmed to ask about your hopes and dreams (and actually *remember* what you tell him), female customers have been coming out of the woodwork.[252]

So, are sexbots for sex, or companionship? Carnal or emotional fulfillment? The answer, of course, is both. RealDolls will have a variety of appeals to people with a variety of appetites. But can the company's marketing efforts address them all?

Perhaps they don't need to. While the promo video racked up a paltry 100,000 views in its first three months on YouTube, *Engadget* videos about RealDolls boast 3.3 million and *VICE* and CNET tack on another 500,000. With a product this controversial and cutting-edge, the press often does the bulk of the heavy promotional lifting. All the RealDoll company needs to do is keep the interviews coming, and let potential customers decide for themselves if they want a friend-with-benefits or just ... benefits.

FAD OF NOTE: SEXBOTS REPLACING SEX WORKERS

"[Sex with robots] has its own taboo still so people can have a feeling that you have to be really weird for that to be the thing that you are into," says San Diego-based family therapist David A. Peters, MFT. "But let's keep in mind that only one generation ago sex toys were only for perverts, and now they are advertised and marketed in magazines." [253]

Further proof that intimacy with machinery is becoming gradually normalized: Sexbots aren't just mail-ordered commodities anymore. They're out in public, stealing jobs from strippers and sex workers. (OK, I'm exaggerating just a bit. But hear me out. Because this is gooooood.)

In January of 2018—in the thick of the International Consumer Electronics Show (CES) in Las Vegas—Sapphire Gentlemen's Club pitted pole-dancing robots against actual, living, professional pole dancers in the event that made global waves. British artist Giles Walker created the dancers who, unlike Harmony X, look very much like machines; cameras for heads, exposed wiring, but molded plastic boobs and derriere of course. Sapphire commissioned the bots to drum up business during CES and readily acknowledged that it was a publicity stunt. But Walker maintains that cyborg pole dancers might eventually have a permanent place in the strip club circuit since erotic robots are a draw for a certain customer.[254]

"Las Vegas is a very competitive environment, and everyone is looking to pull in the customers in whatever way works so I'm sure it'll happen," Giles insisted.

Scoot across the pond to Dortmund, Germany, and you can visit Bordoll, a brothel that offers customers the services of 13 female sex dolls and one male doll. (Live sex workers are available, too, for vanilla customers.) And these are not AI-equipped dolls, just the inert, old-fashioned kind, although owner Evelyn Schwarz has invested in a variety of body types, hair colors, and facial expressions.[255] She charges nearly $100 an hour for a romp with one of her girls. And who, exactly, patronizes Bordoll?

"We get a huge range of people," Schwarz explains. "From 18- to 80-year-olds, from unemployed people to prominent judges."[256]

Initially, she ran her establishment as a regular brothel and BDSM studio, but in April of 2017, she brought the dolls into the rotation. At first, they could only be booked for Sunday sessions, but soon customer demand was so high that they got a whopping six full-time rooms. And business continues to boom. She estimates that one-third of her guests are just curious to find out what it's like to have sex with a doll, but more than two-thirds enjoy their experience so much that they become regular customers. Schwarz maintains that Bordoll creates a safe place for people (mainly men) to act out their fantasies, or try out porn-inspired techniques with a partner incapable of objecting. But she acknowledges that her customers can also be deeply shy or socially awkward people, as well as folks who are fed up with sexual reciprocity.[257]

"Their wives or girlfriends have their own needs, while a prostitute in a brothel has limits on what they will and won't do, sexually," she says. "But our dolls do everything they want, in any position they like."[258]

And at a price that's far lower than ponying up for their own high-quality doll; Schwarz sinks about $2,500 into each of hers.[259]

Fascinating, right? Sure, live sex workers will have their deal-breakers, but there are always specialists. No matter what you want to do, there's *someone* out there willing to do it with you ... for a price. And yet bots and dolls continue to gain ground on their living competition. Perhaps the appeal is simply something new and wildly different. Or perhaps our tolerance of social niceties has already eroded to the point that paying a live person to service our sexual needs feels too onerous. Perhaps we're tired of each other, and just want someone/something that acquiesces and pleases without objection or question.

And perhaps that kind of thinking will lead us down some seriously dark and winding paths. I guess we'll find out.

THE FUTURE OF SEX (AND SEX MARKETING)

"For years I have seen hand-wringing over 'VR sex,' 'sexbots,' high-definition porn, even sexting," Rademacher says. "There's always some new technology coming out that people worry will permanently change the wiring of our brains, or suck the empathy right out of any human that touches them moving us forward into a dark, lonely version of 'The Jetsons.' Will people want to marry robots now? Or worse, will they forego marrying their robots and just have casual sex with them?"

We want to believe we're more evolved, but at our cores, we still feel confused and overwhelmed. We want to adopt the attitude of thoroughly modern sexually knowledgeable adults, but inside we're still middle-schoolers. We titter at ads for Cialis because *why are those people sitting in separate bathtubs,* and sign up for classes about how to talk to our kids about sex. (Tip: they already know, but what they've learned comes from softcore porn they show to each other on the bus ride to middle school.)

As marketers, we've been targeting the bookends of heterosexual sex and sacred innocence. But the reality is proving the world a much more diverse place, and if you've learned anything from this book, I bet you know where that diversity lives.

Yep, you guessed it: in the middle.

The future of sex isn't about the act itself. That's too mechanical, too prescribed, and too physical. The future is about education and products that enable shared pleasure moments; it's a middle path that enables better communication and more understanding between partners—whatever their gender identity or sexual prefer-ence. The middle path is healthier, and it's gaining on us.

Just look at Amazon. We've already determined if it's there, it's headed for the mainstream. Stock up on a Master Series Taint Teaser Silicone Cock Ring and Taint Stimulator, with Amazon Prime you can have it in just two days. Then again, maybe you're more in the mood for a Head Glans Ring with 2 Pressure Joy Balls—use it alone or with a partner, no one's keeping score! Whatever your pleasure, there are plenty of user reviews to peruse while making up your mind. No need to slink off to the back corner of a store or dial 976 numbers to satisfy your cravings; let the freak flag fly. If you're on the 'gram, load up a video and tell us all about it on IGTV.[260]

Sex isn't defined by gender identity or expression—in fact, the concepts of sex, pleasure, and love get equal stage time in the middle ground. Take, for example, pansexuality. Teen Vogue—which in recent years has rapidly proven itself a source of "woke" journalism for young women—asserts that "sexuality is complicated, and the best way we can really understand ourselves and each other is to be more aware of the many different ways humans can love."[261]

Sex isn't just a young person's game. Marketers at the AARP are normalizing pleasure over the act with articles that describe how "Even when these mechanics and dynamics make intercourse impossible, however, sex can remain remarkably fulfilling. Despite the changes aging invariably brings, couples open to erotic alternatives will discover that they can still attain sexual satisfaction together." [262]

So how will marketers shape the next age of sex, sexual understanding, and pleasure? With data, of course.

The data you provide through your shopping preferences and social experiences, the private messages you send through Gmail accounts that get tracked and stored and sold for re-targeting, the information companies collect and sell about your personal life—including all that's captured by devices that continually 'listen" for their cues—will help marketers shape and modify sex into an experience that's better for all humans and the society they live in.

Here's one thing to watch for: assisted sexual pleasure for people we typically don't like to think of as sexual. Oh yeah, you know what I'm talking about. OLDER people. We've long suspected that those people in assisted living are up to no good, and the truth is out there. Just Google "Senior Sex Tips" and you'll find an assortment of advice from sources like Mayo Clinic, SeniorPlanet.org and ah yes, the "Bad Girl's Bible." But despite what the web tells us, we also know some seniors still just can't get enough. And with physical challenges like lower hormones, less flexibility and differing levels of desire, where's a sassy senior to go? In a nursing home or assisted living, nookie still happens. But the pickins' are slim. Places like Germany are already hard at work on it.

In 2017, nursing policy spokeswoman of Germany's Green party Elisabeth Scharfenberg proposed that government fund sexual assistance programs for the elderly.[263] The idea of state-sponsored sexy time raises some eyebrows (among other things?), although some German prostitutes are already offering "sexual assistance" as a line item of options available to nursing home patients.[264] Scharfenberg also pointed to the fact that a working model exists in the Netherlands, where patients have to prove eligibility for state-sponsored relief they can't achieve themselves. Oh, the humanity!

Essentially, the idea of sexual assistance isn't about getting your freak on with a stranger. It boils down to compassion and humanity, getting back to the idea that sexuality and desire happen on a spectrum instead of extremes. As American society moves away from the rigid definitions and expectations of a binary gender system, we'll also start to see more products and services designed for, and marketed to, that spectrum.

Seniors aren't the only ones on the spectrum. Sensual Solutions in Vancouver, Canada was launched in 2011 as a sexual health service for the disabled. Founder Trish St. John explains on sensualsolutions.ca, "I discovered that disabled adults, and parents of adult children with special needs and disabilities, were in search of a service that would help them; but there was nothing specifically designed that was available...Why would we marginalize and shut-out a whole group of people based on being differently-abled? Is there an addendum to Maslow's Hierarchy of Needs that says, "except for those who's [sic] bodies don't function the same as ours?" Basic human rights include all humans regardless of gender, sexual orientation, race, religion, disability or challenge." If you take the time to browse the website, you'll see the company offers Intimacy Coaches whose services range from cuddling and coffee to playing with sex toys, fantasy exploration, basic skin to skin contact and tantric sex. It's about intimacy, human contact and pleasure of all sorts. And whatever your age, ability, gender preference or identity, we all deserve it.

Rademacher is totally on board, saying, "I wish that services like Sensual Solutions would be more available in the U.S. Our laws and general cultural shame around sexuality really get in the way. Many people freak out about the idea that people might pay for comfort, touch, intimacy, or sexual connection. In all the panic we forget that desiring touch is very human and often our most meaningful experiences take place in connection with others."

She also points out that sexual activity isn't just about fun and pleasure; it can be transformative.

"When I've heard stories from people who provide or use services like the ones Sensual Solutions provides, it is clear they are having profound and healing experiences," Rademacher explains. "Our shame-based mindset in the U.S. wants to frame this issue as being about lust, getting off, or people being used. What I hear is totally different: human connection, vulnerability, and discovery of self."

This is the middle path for sex: no more blinders and narrow definitions, and no more either/or marketing and product development. Why would we do that when we can look at the data and discern the vast range of pleasure, desire, kinks, and yearnings that turn people on—or simply make them feel more human?

You can have your sex robot and bone it too. You can also have a cuddle that makes you feel warm and loved and accepted. Or, if you prefer, here's a piece of rubber jewelry for your taint. It doesn't matter what you call yourself, what you look like, or whether you're paralyzed from the neck down. Sex is about to get a lot more fulfilling because marketers finally have the data to know what people want. And oh, boy. They're gonna give it to you... good.

EPILOGUE

MORE HAPPY ENDINGS AHEAD

Here's the tough part about writing a book like this: Every day—no, every *hour*—we're drawing closer to that middle path. Companies are casting off extreme views and tactics and embracing data-driven compromise. It's right there for everyone to see:

"Sonic blends beef and mushrooms for more eco-friendly burger." - CBS News, March 2018[265]

"A tiny German startup that makes protein beer is taking off after winning the country's largest fitness lair"
  - Business Insider, May 2018[266]

"Menu of the Future: Insects, Weeds, and Bleeding Veggie Burgers" - National Geographic, March 2018[267]

"AI Sex dolls are Driving China's Sexual Revolution"
  - Vice News, January 2018[268]

"Artificial Intelligence Already Revolutionizing Pharma"
  - PharmExec.com January 2018[269]

Did you catch those last two? Artificial intelligence (AI)—which many non-Luddites STILL see as a technology on the far horizon—is a factor in multiple industries. Right now. And sure, I fear a robot-led coup as much as the next guy, but I also recognize that AI isn't just Battlestar cylons or Westworld hosts. It takes multiple forms, many of which will prove crucial to landing on the middle path.

Know who else recognizes that? Marketers. Many of whom are already employing AI to worm their way into our hearts, minds, and data.

Yes please AND no thank you

In August of 2017, media company SYZYGY launched a digital insight survey polling 2,000 Americans on their views of artificial intelligence and, specifically, its use in marketing efforts. Once the results were in and analyzed, the company's consumer psychologist, Dr. Paul Marsden, said, "This research reveals how consumers are conflicted when it comes to AI—many see advantages, but there are underlying fears based on whether this technology, or the organizations behind it, has their best interests at heart. Whether marketing AI or marketing *with* AI, brands need to be sensitive to how people feel about this new technology."[270]

Brands are trying to be sensitive, but marketers are antsy. They know that utilizing AI to tease out consumer insights might scare a few folks, *but so what?* The payload of priceless consumer data will be worth a few freaked-out oldsters.

- SYZYGY's research found that 78% of polled Americans were in favor of a "Blade Runner Law": legislation that would make it illegal for AI applications including social media bots, chatbots, and virtual assistants to pose as media bots, chatbots, and virtual assistants to pose as actual humans.[271] Marketers would likely fight this tooth-and-nail since their client companies use bots to handle everything from simple customer service requests to ongoing consumer research.

- In 2017, Pew Research reported that the majority of Americans are extremely wary of driverless cars.[272] Marketers, on the other hand, salivate because "the spread of driverless cars will bring a new advertising platform where people whose attention is no longer needed for driving will start engaging in a range of other activities as they ride."[273]
- A 2018 Gallup poll found that 73% of respondents fear that AI will eliminate jobs.[274] Marketers are (bizarrely) already handing over *their own jobs* to bots: in 2015, ad agency McCann Japan decided to program an all-AI creative director. In 2017, the company pitted the AI creative director against a human creative director in a contest to design the best ad for client company Mondelez. According to the 100 ad execs who judged the entries, the AI creative director won.[275]

So, while the public is hesitant, the marketing industry is fully on-board deploying AI as often as it can.

Andrew Stephen—L'Oréal Professor of Marketing & Associate Dean of Research at Oxford University's Saïd Business School—believes that merging marketing with AI will only lead to good things. For everyone.

"Marketers have more insights-related tools at their disposal that facilitate true data-driven decision making, but AI is needed to help integrate across tools, datasets, and platforms," he said in a *Forbes* article. "Of course, data are never perfect and marketers' interpretations of patterns found in data by machine learning and AI analytics systems are still subject to bias and could mislead. However, we have never had so many opportunities for truly data-driven marketing."[276]

Neil Davidson, managing director and partner of London-based marketing agency Hey, Human, takes the logic a step further. He thinks that brands need to take the reins and help make AI less scary and more approachable.

"Branding exists to put a human face to a product, and we've been making 'stuff' resonate on an emotional level for decades. Emotional intelligence [EI] is arguably the future of AI," he wrote in an opinion piece for *More About Advertising.* "By integrating tracking software that detects our emotions via facial expressions, eye movements, voice and heart rates, a machine can respond in a more emotionally articulate and intelligent way. Brands need to get the dynamic right in an increasingly automated world. We need to work with new concepts to help develop technology that is both empathetic and intuitive to human need."[277]

News flash: I agree. Marketing exists to sell stuff to people, but the best possible way to do that is by knowing what they want to begin with (or hell... how about modifying their behavior to want it?!) Artificial intelligence is the bridge between consumer need and marketer desire, connecting both on a mutually beneficial middle path. But, here's something that's worth a big pause:

There will be a few nasty side-effects.

AI, THE GREAT ENABLER.

Not that long ago, "bingeing" was bad. It was something folks with eating disorders struggled with, and something college kids embraced beer-wise. Bingeing meant overdoing it, eating or drinking to the point of sickness, cramming so much of something into your system that it hit overload.

Bingeing is STILL bad ... we just pretend it's not. The evil masterminds at Netflix spawned the "binge-watch," and now mainlining media of all kinds has been normalized. People binge-read comics, binge-play video games, binge-listen to podcasts, consume entire series of novels in the space of a few days. This is on top of the binge eating, drinking, smoking, pill-popping, and screwing that has been going on all along. The difference is that some of the cultural stigmas have eased up; bingeing isn't a sign of being ill or out-of-control, it's cute and cuddly. Something you do, curled up on the couch with friends.

Which means we're all primed to become obsessive, addicted, binge-happy zombies across all fronts. And AI is gonna help.

Scientists at Johns Hopkins University found that binge behavior can be triggered by external stimuli: just hearing the chimes of an ice cream truck can spark overeating, and just seeing a little mound of white powder can catalyze a cocaine-snorting spree.[278] This means that—in our increasingly digitized and media-addicted world—all marketers need to do is systematically trigger us, and we'll buy, eat, drink, or watch whatever they want us to. Artificial intelligence will do the legwork of learning how to initiate human binge behavior, then analyze which things we should be bingeing. Bots will follow us wherever we surf, pushing triggering stimuli and nudging us toward excess.

It's going to be one helluva drunken digital revelry.

And then! Guess who's going to swoop in and save us from our depraved, strung-out, binge-driven little selves? Why AI, of course.

Scientists and programmers are already using machine learning to track and catalog our obsessive behaviors, and in some cases, reverse them. Dr. Lisa A. Marsch, director of the Dartmouth Center for Technology and Behavioral Health, has advocated for the use of tech-based interventions for both preventing and treating substance abuse in teens.[279] UNC Charlotte scientists trained a neural network to identify social media posts related to binge-drinking.[280] Researchers from Worcester Polytechnic Institute and the University of Connecticut developed a smartphone app that utilized AI to predict user eating patterns AND provide potential interventions to prevent binge activity.[281]

It's already happening. This technology is going to be our disease and our cure. *Brace yourselves.*

So, what do we do?

Well, nothing. I'm not saying you have to do anything.

Remember when you were a kid and your parents taught you to be aware of the world around you? (Let's hope so, at least.) One of your earliest lessons was probably, "Look both ways before crossing the street," and that kind of awareness still applies today. Know your surroundings—I'm talking about the physical world as well as online.

This book offers the same advice: understand the world and be aware of its dangers. Make good choices. Look both ways before you hand off your data to some faceless mega-corporation. Acknowledge that what you say and do is being monitored, and may be used against you. You can't avoid all marketing, social media, computer use, or communication in general unless you're destined for the Hermitage ... but you can be an informed participant. And that may minimize the amount of involuntary manipulation you encounter.

In fact, if you tune in to how your information is being collected and used, you can even learn to manipulate it right back.

At the very least, you can change how you use the web itself. Privacy-focused search engine DuckDuckGo offers an app and browser extensions that block advertising as well as your search activity from companies that would otherwise follow you around the web. (I'm looking at you, Google and Facebook.) All I'm saying is change your behavior to be more guarded, but work to your advantage; there's no big warning.

Manage your own destiny. Keep an open mind. That's how I see it because there's just no stopping it.

Join me for the ride.

We've had some good times in these pages, you and me. Talked about some cool brands. Disturbing trends. Notable campaigns. Now, tell me you never set the book aside, took a minute, and tapped a brand or phrase into your mobile device to take a deeper gander at one of the topics.

Yeah, knew you did. *Captivating, isn't it?* It's the kind of stuff that sends you down a rabbit hole.

Which is why I've prepared some rabbit holes especially for you over at *TheFADSBook.com*. Each chapter has its own section with more links to the articles, campaigns, and images we talked about here. And on the blog, you can join me for the ride with a never-ending stream of brain-bending-breakthroughs and updates. We'll catch the stories and updates that build on FADS marketing, and we'll watch it all unfold together.

There's no stopping it. You're already part of it, and you know you want it.

- Tony

CITATIONS

[1] Foxcroft, Louise. "I Wonder - How We Fought Fat throughout History." BBC, January 15, 2015, www.bbc.co.uk/timelines/z9nfyrd.

[2] Winston, Kimberly. "Gluttony and the Seven Deadly Sins." Religion News Service, November 22, 2017, www.religionnews.com/2016/11/22/the-splainer-gluttony-and-the-seven-deadly-sins.

[3] Wolchover, Natalie. "The Real Skinny: Expert Traces America's Thin Obsession." LiveScience, Purch, January 26, 2012, www.livescience.com/18131-women-thin-dieting-history.html.

[4] Jez, Mojca. "Molecular Gastronomy – The Food Science." Splice, September 24, 2015, https://splice-bio.com/molecular-gastronomy-the-food-science.

[5] Rosenthal, Robert. "5 Psychological Tactics Marketers Use To Influence Consumer Behavior." Fast Company, 7 July 2014, www.fastcompany.com/3032675/5-psychological-tactics-marketers-

use-to-influence-consumer-behavior. and Leonidou, Leonidas C., and Constantinos N. Leonidou. Rational Versus Emotional Appeals in Newspaper Advertising: Copy, Art, and Layout Differences, 15:4, 522-546. Journal of Promotion Management, 2009.

[6] Wood, Orlando. "How Emotional Tugs Trump Rational Pushes." The Journal of Advertising Research, March 1, 2012, www.journalofadvertisingresearch.com/content/52/1/31.

[7] Pringle, Hamish. "Why Emotional Messages Beat Rational Ones." Ad Age, March 2, 2009, adage.com/article/cmo-strategy/emotional-messages-beat-rational/134920.

[8] Zazzi, Jason. "Five Highly Emotional Ads That Went Viral In 2015." Forbes, December 17, 2015, www.forbes.com/sites/onmarketing/2015/12/17/five-highly-emotional-ads-that-went-viral-in-2015.

[9] "OCE | U.S. Food Waste Challenge | FAQ's." USDA. https://www.usda.gov/oce/foodwaste/faqs.htm.

[10] Gianatasio, Dave. "Follow a Strawberry From Birth to Grave in This Oddly Emotional Ad About Food Waste." Adweek, April 20, 2016, http://www.adweek.com/creativity/follow-strawberry-birth-grave-oddly-emotional-ad-about-food-waste-170930.

[11] Gianatasio, Dave. "Follow a Strawberry From Birth to Grave in This Oddly Emotional Ad About Food Waste." Adweek, April 20, 2016, http://www.adweek.com/creativity/follow-strawberry-birth-grave-oddly-emotional-ad-about-food-waste-170930.

[12] Hunt, Kristin. "Looking Back on 58yrs of McDonald's Slogans." Thrillist, September 2, 2013, https://www.thrillist.com/eat/nation/looking-back-on-58yrs-of-mcdonalds-slogans.

[13] Garcia, Ahiza. "Coca-Cola Slogans through the Years." CNNMoney, January 19, 2016, http://money.cnn.com/2016/01/19/news/companies/coca-cola-slogans/index.html.

[14] Hilton, Kyle. "The Science of Sensory Marketing." Harvard Business Review, March 2015, https://hbr.org/2015/03/the-science-of-sensory-marketing.

[15] Chodosh, Sara. "There's No Such Thing as Naturally Orange Cheese." Popular Science, February 16, 2018, https://www.popsci.com/why-is-some-cheese-orange.

[16] Chodosh, Sara. "There's No Such Thing as Naturally Orange Cheese." Popular Science, February 16, 2018, https://www.popsci.com/why-is-some-cheese-orange.

[17] Chodosh, Sara. "There's No Such Thing as Naturally Orange Cheese." Popular Science, February 16, 2018, https://www.popsci.com/why-is-some-cheese-orange.

[18] "Red Leicester." Cheese.com - World's Greatest Cheese Resource, https://www.cheese.com/red-leicester.

[19] Rhodes, Jesse. "Food Dye Origins: When Margarine Was Pink." Smithsonian.com, April 7, 2011, www.smithsonianmag.com/arts-culture/food-dye-origins-when-margarine-was-pink-175950936.

[20] Chodosh, Sara. "There's No Such Thing as Naturally Orange Cheese." Popular Science, February 16, 2018, www.popsci.com/why-is-some-cheese-orange.

[21] "About Us." History | McCain USA Foodservice, 2018, www.mccainusafoodservice.com/About.

22 McCabe, Maisie. "McCain Cooks up Potato-Scented Bus Stop Campaign." Campaign US, February 7, 2012, www.campaignlive.com/article/mccain-cooks-potato-scented-bus-stop-campaign/1115738.

23 Gaines Lewis, Jordan. "Smells Ring Bells: How Smell Triggers Memories and Emotions." Psychology Today, Sussex Publishers, January 12, 2015, www.psychologytoday.com/blog/brain-babble/201501/smells-ring-bells-how-smell-triggers-memories-and-emotions.

24 Hemsley, Steve. "Top Sensory Marketing Trends for 2016." Marketing Week, January 18, 2016, www.marketingweek.com/2016/01/18/top-sensory-marketing-trends-for-2016.

25 Annear, Steve. "Dunkin' Donuts Sprays the Smell of Coffee Onto Buses to Increase Sales [Video]." Americaninno.com, July 24, 2012, www.americaninno.com/boston/dunkin-donuts-sprays-the-smell-of-coffee-onto-buses-to-increase-sales-video.

26 Yoon, Eddie. "The Grocery Industry Confronts a New Problem: Only 10% of Americans Love Cooking." Harvard Business Review, September 22, 2017, hbr.org/2017/09/the-grocery-industry-confronts-a-new-problem-only-10-of-americans-love-cooking.

27 Miller, Noah. "17% Of U.S. Adults Purchase Meal Kit Delivery Services." Meal Kit Delivery Services, July 13, 2017, www.packagedfacts.com/Content/Blog/2017/07/13/17-of-Adults-Receive-Meal-Kit-Delivery-.

28 Shontell, Alyson. "How 3 Guys Created Blue Apron, a $2 Billion Recipe-Delivery Business with 2,500 Employees, in 36 Months." Business Insider, October 19, 2015, www.businessinsider.com/blue-apron-founder-story-sai-100-2015-10.

[29] Kell, John. "Meals in the Mail: How Blue Apron Got Started and Where It's Heading." Fortune, September 11, 2016, fortune.com/2016/09/11/blue-apron-meal-delivery.

[30] "Blue Apron Cuts Marketing Budget and Customer Count Drops." Ad Age, August 10, 2017, adage.com/article/cmo-strategy/blue-apron-cuts-marketing-budget-customer-count-drops/310085.

31 Pankaew, Derek. "An In-Depth Look at Blue Apron's $100 Million Marketing Strategy." Marketing Strategy, December 12, 2017, www.marketingstrategy.com/blue-apron-marketing-strategy.

[32] "Blue Apron Holdings, Inc. Form S-1." SEC.gov, June 1, 2017, www.sec.gov/Archives/edgar/data/1701114/000104746917003765/a2232259zs-1.htm.

[33] de la Merced, Michael J. "Blue Apron Pursues I.P.O. as Amazon Looms Over Industry." The New York Times, June 19, 2017, www.nytimes.com/2017/06/19/business/dealbook/blue-apron-ipo.html.

[34] "Blue Apron Cuts Marketing Budget and Customer Count Drops." Ad Age, August 10, 2017, adage.com/article/cmo-strategy/blue-apron-cuts-marketing-budget-customer-count-drops/310085.

[35] Hirsch, Lauren, and Angela Moon. "Meal-Kit Maker Blue Apron Goes Public, Demand Underwhelms as Amazon..." Reuters, June 28, 2017, www.reuters.com/article/us-blueapron-ipo/meal-kit-maker-blue-apron-goes-public-demand-underwhelms-as-amazon-looms-idUSKBN19J1C5.

[36] "Coconut Flour Market Taxonomy By End Use – Industrial, Retail (Modern Trade, Grocery/Conventional Stores, E-Retailers); By Application – Baked Products (Bread, Cookies, Cakes),Snack Foods (Multi-Grain Chips, Polvoron, Kroepeck, Extruded Products), Extruded

Products, Animal Feed; By Product Form – Whole Full Fat Flour, Low Fat High Fibre Flour, Medium Fat Flour; By Technology – Fresh-Dry Process, Wet Process; By Nature – Conventional, Organic." Future Market Insights, May 22, 2017, www.futuremarketinsights.com/reports/coconut-flour-market

[37] Ask Umbra®. "Are Coconut Products Bad for the Environment?" Grist, November 25, 2016, grist.org/food/are-coconut-products-bad-for-the-environment.

[38] "Behind the Seal - Fair Trade News." Fair Trade Certified, 2018, www.fairtradecertified.org/news.

[39] American College of Allergy, Asthma, and Immunology. "21 percent increase in childhood peanut allergy since 2010: More children have food allergies, including more black children." ScienceDaily, October 27, 2017, www.sciencedaily.com/releases/2017/10/171027085541.htm

[40] Ferdman, Roberto A. "The Rise of the American Almond Craze in One Nutty Chart." The Washington Post, August 6, 2014, www.washingtonpost.com/news/wonk/wp/2014/08/06/the-rise-of-the-american-almond-craze-in-one-nutty-chart/?utm_term=.8e81541450ac.

[41] Hamblin, James. "The Dark Side of Almond Use." The Atlantic, August 28, 2014, www.theatlantic.com/health/archive/2014/08/almonds-demon-nuts/379244.

[42] Watson, Elaine. "Almonds Are on Fire, Says Blue Diamond CEO as Meteoric Growth Rates Continue." Foodnavigator-Usa.com, March 25, 2014, www.foodnavigator-usa.com/Article/2014/03/25/Almonds-are-on-fire-says-Blue-Diamond-CEO-as-meteoric-growth-rates-continue.

[43] Stanley, T.L. "A Tasty Nut Butter Breaks Jelly's Heart in Tragicomic Ads for MaraNatha." Adweek, September 18, 2017, www.adweek.com/brand-marketing/a-tasty-nut-butter-breaks-jellys-heart-in-tragicomic-ads-for-maranatha.

[44] Ferdman, Roberto A. "The Rise of the American Almond Craze in One Nutty Chart." The Washington Post, August 6, 2014, www.washingtonpost.com/news/wonk/wp/2014/08/06/the-rise-of-the-american-almond-craze-in-one-nutty-chart/?utm_term=.8e81541450ac.

[45] Philpott, Tom. "Lay off the Almond Milk, You Ignorant Hipsters." Mother Jones, July 16, 2014, www.motherjones.com/food/2014/07/lay-off-almond-milk-ignorant-hipsters.

[46] Philpott, Tom. "Lay off the Almond Milk, You Ignorant Hipsters." Mother Jones, July 16, 2014, www.motherjones.com/food/2014/07/lay-off-almond-milk-ignorant-hipsters.

[47] Bowes, Peter. "Why Are Almonds so Expensive?" BBC News, February 12, 2014, www.bbc.com/news/magazine-26118225.

[48] "2017 Trend Insight" FONA International, 2017, http://www.fona.com/wp-content/uploads/2018/02/SnackingIndulgenceTrendInsight_0117.pdf

[49] Foodmix Marketing Communications. "New Research Reveals Indulgence Has Reached America's Healthiest Eaters." PR Newswire: News Distribution, Targeting and Monitoring, February 14, 2018, www.prnewswire.com/news-releases/new-research-reveals-indulgence-has-reached-americas-healthiest-eaters-300597130.html.

[50] Richards, Katie. "New Oreo Campaign Reminds You How Delightful Dunking Cookies Can Be." Ad Week, February 8, 2017,

http://www.adweek.com/brand-marketing/new-oreo-campaign-reminds-you-how-delightful-dunking-cookies-can-be/

51 Mars. "Hungry Meme." Tumblr, 2016, www.tumblr.com/tagged/snickers?before=263554953.

52 O'Connor, Anahad. "The Claim: Chocolate Is an Aphrodisiac." The New York Times, July, 18 2006, www.nytimes.com/2006/07/18/health/18real.html.

53 Sandler, Emma. "Magnum Ice Cream Delivers A Luxuriously Sweet Treat This Summer With Moschino." Forbes, July 11 2017, www.forbes.com/sites/emmasandler/2017/07/11/magnum-icecream-moschino-jeremy-scott-cara-delevingne.

54 Nichols, JamesMichael. "Magnum Wants You To 'Be True To Your Pleasure' -- No Matter What Your Gender." The Huffington Post, February 2, 2016, www.huffingtonpost.com/2015/05/27/magnum-gender-nonconforming_n_7452430.html.

55 Magnum. "Selling Pleasure, Not Ice Cream." Coloribus.com, March 2011, www.coloribus.com/adsarchive/promo-casestudy/magnum-selling-pleasure-not-ice-cream-16781705.

56 Rabasca Roepe, Lisa. "The Diet Industry." SAGE Business Researcher, March 5. 2018, businessresearcher.sagepub.com/sbr-1946-105904-2881576/20180305/the-diet-industry.

57 Zacks Equity Research. "NutriSystem (NTRI) Adopts Multi-Brand Strategy for 2018." NASDAQ.com, December 28, 2017, www.nasdaq.com/article/nutrisystem-ntri-adopts-multi-brand-strategy-for-2018-cm897800.

58 Fain, Jean. "In 'Eating Lab,' A Psychologist Spills Secrets On Why Diets Fail." NPR, June 1, 2015,

www.npr.org/sections/thesalt/2015/06/01/411217634/in-eating-lab-psychologist-spills-secrets-on-why-diets-fail.

⁵⁹ "Nutrisystem Poised to Expand via Multi-Brand Strategy for Diet Season 2018." Business Wire, December 26, 2017, www.businesswire.com/news/home/20171226005131/en/Nutrisystem-Poised-Expand-Multi-Brand-Strategy-Diet-Season.

⁶⁰ "Nutrisystem Tumbles After Diet-Season Marketing Campaign Flops." Ad Age, February 26, 2018, adage.com/article/cmo-strategy/nutrisystem-tumbles-diet-marketing-campaign-flops/312524.

⁶¹ "Nutrisystem Falls Sharply on Poor Q1 Guidance as Co Unable to Draw in Enough New Customers (NTRI)." Briefing.com, February 27, 2018, www.briefing.com/investor/analysis/story-stocks/nutrisystem-falls-sharply-on-poor-q1-guidance-as-co-unable-to-draw-in-enough-new-customers-(ntri).htm.

⁶² "Nutrisystem Falls Sharply on Poor Q1 Guidance as Co Unable to Draw in Enough New Customers (NTRI)." Briefing.com, February 27, 2018, www.briefing.com/investor/analysis/story-stocks/nutrisystem-falls-sharply-on-poor-q1-guidance-as-co-unable-to-draw-in-enough-new-customers-(ntri).htm.

⁶³ Roberts, Michelle. "'Seductive Names' Make Vegetables More Appealing." BBC News, June 13, 2017, www.bbc.com/news/health-40245922.

⁶⁴ Weiner, Rachel. "The New York City Soda Ban Explained." The Washington Post, March 11, 2013, www.washingtonpost.com/news/the-fix/wp/2013/03/11/the-new-york-city-soda-ban-explained.

⁶⁵ "Noble Eightfold Path." Wikipedia, August 5, 2018, en.wikipedia.org/wiki/Noble_Eightfold_Path.

[66] "Pea Protein." Eat This Much, 2018, www.eatthismuch.com/food/view/pea-protein,6629.

[67] Andrews, A.J. "Soy Flour as a Hamburger Extender." Healthy Eating | SF Gate, June 11, 2018, healthyeating.sfgate.com/soy-flour-hamburger-extender-11570.html.

[68] True Food Kitchen, 2018, www.truefoodkitchen.com.

[69] Goldstein, Joelle. "Oprah Winfrey Invests in Healthy Restaurant Chain True Food Kitchen." The Hollywood Reporter, July 11, 2018, www.hollywoodreporter.com/news/oprah-winfrey-invests-healthy-restaurant-true-food-kitchen-1126342.

[70] "Controlled Substance Schedules." DEA Diversion Control Division, www.deadiversion.usdoj.gov/schedules.

[71] Lopez, German. "The War on Drugs, Explained." Vox, May 8, 2016, www.vox.com/cards/war-on-drugs-marijuana-cocaine-heroin-meth/war-on-drugs-international-treaties.

[72] Smith, David E. and Skalnik, J. Robert,"Changing Patterns in the Consumption of Alcoholic Beverages in Europe and the United States.", E - European Advances in Consumer Research Volume 2, eds. Flemming Hansen, Provo, UT : Association for Consumer Research, 1995, Pages: 343-355.

[73] "Total alcoholic beverage sales in the United States from 2006 to 2016 (in million U.S. dollars)." Statista, www.statista.com/statistics/207936/us-total-alcoholic-beverages-sales-since-1990.

[74] "Alcohol Advertising." Federal Trade Commission Consumer Information, September 2013, www.consumer.ftc.gov/articles/0391-alcohol-advertising.

[75] Stephenson, Steve. "Alcohol Advertising and Youth." Johns Hopkins Bloomberg School of Public Health, April 2007, www.camy.org/resources/fact-sheets/alcohol-advertising-and-youth/index.html.

[76] "Whiskey and America: A Post-Prohibition Reunion (Fortune, 1933)." Fortune, June 24, 2012, fortune.com/2012/06/24/whiskey-and-america-a-post-prohibition-reunion-fortune-1933.

[77] Dubois, Shelby. "The New United States of Booze." Fortune, February 19, 2013, fortune.com/2013/02/19/the-new-united-states-of-booze.

[78] "Whiskey and America: A Post-Prohibition Reunion (Fortune, 1933)." Fortune, June 24, 2012, fortune.com/2012/06/24/whiskey-and-america-a-post-prohibition-reunion-fortune-1933.

[79] Schultz., E.J. "Post-Prohibition Hangover: Why Booze Marketers Were Slow to Advertise." Ad Age, December 5, 2013, adage.com/article/news/booze-marketers-slow-advertise-post-prohibition/245534.

[80] Dubois, Shelby. "The New United States of Booze." Fortune, February 19, 2013, fortune.com/2013/02/19/the-new-united-states-of-booze.

[81] Schonbrun, Zach. "Beer Ads That Portray Women as Empowered Consumers, Not Eye Candy." The New York Times, January 31, 2016, https://www.nytimes.com/2016/02/01/business/media/beer-ads-that-portray-women-as-empowered-consumers-not-eye-candy.html?_r=0.

[82] Nurin, Tara. "After Decades Of 'Beer Babe' Commercials, Liquor Ads Could Improve NFL's Gender Relations." Fortune, June 9, 2017, https://www.forbes.com/sites/taranurin/2017/06/09/after-decades-of-

beer-babe-commercials-liquor-ads-could-improve-nfls-gender-relations/#35ee2b5e540e

83 Schonbrun, Zach. "Beer Ads That Portray Women as Empowered Consumers, Not Eye Candy." The New York Times, January 31, 2016, https://www.nytimes.com/2016/02/01/business/media/beer-ads-that-portray-women-as-empowered-consumers-not-eye-candy.html?_r=0.

84 Domonoske, Camila. "Drinking On The Rise In U.S., Especially For Women, Minorities, Older Adults." NPR, August 10, 2017, https://www.npr.org/sections/thetwo-way/2017/08/10/542409957/drinking-on-the-rise-in-u-s-especially-for-women-minorities-older-adults

85 Kindy, Kimberly, and Dan Keating. "For Women, Heavy Drinking Has Been Normalized. That's Dangerous." The Washington Post, December 23, 2016, https://www.washingtonpost.com/national/for-women-heavy-drinking-has-been-normalized-thats-dangerous/2016/12/23/0e701120-c381-11e6-9578-0054287507db_story.html?utm_term=.1dcd9b1dd754.

86 Koerner, Brendan. "The Long, Slow, Torturous Death of Zima." Slate Magazine, November 26, 2008, http://www.slate.com/articles/life/drink/2008/11/the_long_slow_torturous_death_of_zima.html.

87 "ZIMA Is Back - You in or What?" MillerCoors, June 20, 2017, https://www.millercoors.com/News-Center/Latest-News/zima-is-back-you-in-or-what-0.

88 Taylor, Kate. "A Controversial '90s-era Beverage That Was Pulled from Shelves during the Recession Is Back with a Vengeance." Business Insider, June 28, 2017, https://www.businessinsider.com/zima-is-back-after-being-pulled-from-shelves-in-2008-2017-6.

[89] Koerner, Brendan. "The Long, Slow, Torturous Death of Zima."
Slate Magazine, November 26, 2008,
http://www.slate.com/articles/life/drink/2008/11/the_long_slow_tortur
ous_death_of_zima.html.

[90] Koerner, Brendan. "The Long, Slow, Torturous Death of Zima."
Slate Magazine, November 26, 2008,
http://www.slate.com/articles/life/drink/2008/11/the_long_slow_tortur
ous_death_of_zima.html.

[91] Taylor, Kate. "A Controversial '90s-era Beverage That Was Pulled
from Shelves during the Recession Is Back with a Vengeance." Business Insider, June 28, 2017, https://www.businessinsider.com/zima-is-
back-after-being-pulled-from-shelves-in-2008-2017-6.

[92] Sixohsicks. "R/AskReddit - What Did Zima Taste Like?" Reddit,
2016,
https://www.reddit.com/r/AskReddit/comments/3r1ip9/what_did_zim
a_taste_like.

[93] Koerner, Brendan. "The Long, Slow, Torturous Death of Zima."
Slate Magazine, November 26, 2008,
http://www.slate.com/articles/life/drink/2008/11/the_long_slow_tortur
ous_death_of_zima.html.

[94] Koerner, Brendan. "The Long, Slow, Torturous Death of Zima."
Slate Magazine, November 26, 2008,
http://www.slate.com/articles/life/drink/2008/11/the_long_slow_tortur
ous_death_of_zima.html.

[95] Schultz., E.J. "Remember Zima? Clear Malt Beverage Is Poised for
Comeback." Ad Age, February 16, 2017, http://adage.com/article/cmo-
strategy/1990s-clear-malt-beverage-zima-poised-comeback/308013.

96 York, Emily Bryson, and Robert Channick. "Skinnygirl Margarita Deal Shows Women's Buying Power." Los Angeles Times, March 30, 2011, http://articles.latimes.com/2011/mar/30/business/la-fi-skinnygirl-20110330.

97 Kindy, Kimberly, and Dan Keating. "For Women, Heavy Drinking Has Been Normalized. That's Dangerous." The Washington Post, December 23, 2016, https://www.washingtonpost.com/national/for-women-heavy-drinking-has-been-normalized-thats-dangerous/2016/12/23/0e701120-c381-11e6-9578-0054287507db_story.html?utm_term=.1dcd9b1dd754.

98 Slade, Tim, Wendy Swift, Cath Chapman, and Maree Teesson. "Here's Why Women Are Drinking as Much Alcohol as Men." Newsweek, November 8, 2016, http://www.newsweek.com/alcohol-consumption-drunk-women-men-study-gender-gap-516277.

99 Sheinbaum, Hilary. "Skinnygirl Bethenny Frankel on Overcoming Obstacles And Being A Woman In The Spirits Industry." Forbes, January 27, 2018, https://www.forbes.com/sites/hilarysheinbaum/2018/01/25/skinnygirls-bethenny-frankel-on-overcoming-obstacles-and-being-a-woman-in-the-spirits-industry/#1370cf85567f.

100 Berg, Madeline. "Skinnygirl, Fat Wallet: How Bethenny Frankel Earns More Than Any Other Real Housewife." Forbes, November 17, 2016, https://www.forbes.com/sites/maddieberg/2016/11/16/skinnygirl-fat-wallet-how-bethenny-frankel-earns-more-than-any-other-housewife/#4b3eaa3a6311.

101 "Drink Like a Lady: Cocktailing Guide to Ladies' Drinks | Skinny-girl." Skinnygirl Cocktails, https://www.skinnygirlcocktails.com/drink-like-a-lady.

102 Berg, Madeline. "Skinnygirl, Fat Wallet: How Bethenny Frankel

Earns More Than Any Other Real Housewife." Forbes, November 17, 2016, https://www.forbes.com/sites/maddieberg/2016/11/16/skinnygirl-fat-wallet-how-bethenny-frankel-earns-more-than-any-other-housewife/#4b3eaa3a6311.

[103] Pikul, Corie. "The Best Drinks for Dieters." Oprah.com, http://www.oprah.com/health/the-best-drinks-for-dieters-low-calorie-cocktails/all.

[104] "Low Calorie Alcoholic Drinks: Low Cal Drinks | Skinnygirl." Skinnygirl Cocktails, 2015, https://www.skinnygirlcocktails.com.

[105] Bruso, Jessica. "Calories in Flavored Vodka." LIVESTRONG.COM, October 3, 2017, https://www.livestrong.com/article/302365-calories-in-flavored-vodka.

[106] "Low Calorie Alcoholic Drinks: Low Cal Drinks | Skinnygirl." Skinnygirl Cocktails, 2015, https://www.skinnygirlcocktails.com.

[107] Nunley, Kim. "How Many Calories in Rose Wine?" LIVESTRONG.-COM, October 3, 2017, https://www.livestrong.com/article/311692-how-many-calories-in-rose-wine.

[108] "Low Calorie Alcoholic Drinks: Low Cal Drinks | Skinnygirl." Skinnygirl Cocktails, 2015, https://www.skinnygirlcocktails.com.

[109] "Brand Profile: Skinnygirl Has More Fun." Beverage Media Group, September 10, 2012, https://www.beveragemedia.com/2012/09/10/brand-profile-skinnygirl-has-more-fun.

[110] Eber, Hailey. "Why 'Diet Booze' Leaves a Bad Taste in Our Mouths." New York Post. December 26, 2013. https://nypost.com/2013/12/26/just-say-no-to-diet-booze.

[111] Neill, Rob, and Associated Press. "Skinnygirl cocktails are fastest growing liquor brand, report says." NBC News, November 2, 2018, https://www.nbcnews.com/business/markets/skinnygirl-cocktails-are-fastest-growing-liquor-brand-report-says-flna746584.

[112] Maheshwari, Sapna. "Sales Slim Down For Bethenny Frankel's Skinnygirl Cocktail Brand." Buzzfeed, February 5, 2015, https://www.buzzfeed.com/sapna/sales-slim-down-for-bethenny-frankels-skinnygirl-cocktail-br?utm_term=.wv9d9KKij#.yo7KZOOe2.

[113] "The Pendleton Whisky Posse.' Pendleton, 2018, https://pendletonwhisky.com/community/posse/

[114] Oster, Erik. "FCB Chicago Shares Some 'Margarita Moments' in New Bud Light Lime-A-Rita Campaign." AgencySpy, March 14, 2017, https://www.adweek.com/agencyspy/fcb-chicago-shares-some-margarita-moments-in-new-bud-light-lime-a-rita-campaign/127501.

[115] "Jane Walker - Black Label Scotch Whisky | Johnnie Walker." Walk With Us | Scotch Whisky Cocktails & Serves, 2016, https://www.johnniewalker.com/en-us/our-whisky/limited-editions/jane-walker.

[116] "1999: Budweiser airs its 'Wassup' commercial in 1999." The Drum, March 31, 2016, http://www.thedrum.com/news/2016/03/31/1999-budweiser-airs-its-wassup-commercial-1999.

[117] Fulton, Wil. "Holy Crap, Guys. the 'Whassup?!' Commercial Is 17 Years Old." Thrillist, March 6, 2016, https://www.thrillist.com/drink/nation/holy-crap-guys-the-whassup-commercial-is-17-years-old.

[118] Victor, Daniel. "How Do You Turn an Ad Into a Meme? Two Words: Dilly Dilly." The New York Times, December 31, 2017,

https://www.nytimes.com/2017/12/31/business/media/dilly-dilly-bud-light.html.

[119] Victor, Daniel. "How Do You Turn an Ad Into a Meme? Two Words: Dilly Dilly." The New York Times, December 31, 2017, https://www.nytimes.com/2017/12/31/business/media/dilly-dilly-bud-light.html.

[120] Haden, Jeff. " 'Dilly Dilly': A Marketing Expert Analyzes the Highly Successful Bud Light Ad Campaign." Inc., March 21, 2018, https://www.inc.com/jeff-haden/dilly-dilly-a-marketing-expert-analyzes-highly-successful-bud-light-ad-campaign.html.

[121] Flanagan, Graham. "What 'Dilly Dilly' means — and how Bud Light came up with its viral campaign." Business Insider, February 4, 2018, http://www.businessinsider.com/bud-light-dilly-dilly-viral-commercial-super-bowl-campaign-2017-12.

[122] Erickson, Nate. "The Most Interesting Man in the World Is Gone. Long Live the Most Interesting Man in the World." Esquire. March 14, 2018, https://www.esquire.com/food-drink/drinks/a19436369/most-interesting-man-canceled-jonathan-goldsmith.

[123] Wolff-Mann, Ethan. "The Most Interesting Man in the World: Dos Equis Ad's Success | Money." Time. March 9, 2016. http://time.com/money/4252403/success-most-interesting-man-in-the-world-ad.

[124] Schultz, E.J. "Dos Equis Sidelines The Most Interesting Man in the World." Ad Age, March 14, 2018, adage.com/article/cmo-strategy/dos-equis-sidelines-interesting-man-world/312721.

[125] Lapetina, Adam. "The Crazy Stories Behind 8 of the World's Oldest Booze Brands." Thrillist, April 8, 2015, www.thrillist.com/drink/nation/oldest-liquor-in-the-world.

126 "Innovation in Japan: The Exception Becomes the Rule." The Coca-Cola Company, February 22, 2018, www.coca-colacompany.com/stories/innovation-in-japan-the-exception-becomes-the-rule.

127 Corcione, Danielle. "Coca-Cola Wants to Get You Drunk." Complex, March 7, 2018, www.complex.com/life/2018/03/coca-cola-wants-to-get-you-drunk.

128 "Coca-Cola to Launch Alcoholic Drink." The Irish Times, March 7, 2018, www.irishtimes.com/business/agribusiness-and-food/coca-cola-to-launch-alcoholic-drink-1.3418021.

129 Buehler, Nathan. "Top 5 Companies Owned By Coca Cola (KO)." Investopedia, October 25, 2017, www.investopedia.com/articles/markets/011216/top-5-companies-owned-coca-cola-ko.asp.

130 Coca-Cola Co.: Ad Spend 2017 | Statistic." Statista, February 2018, www.statista.com/statistics/286526/coca-cola-advertising-spending-worldwide.

131 O'Malley Greenburg, Zack. "The Real Story Behind Jay Z's Champagne Deal." Forbes, November 6, 2014, www.forbes.com/sites/zackomalleygreenburg/2014/11/06/why-jay-zs-champagne-news-isnt-so-new.

132 How Jay-Z And Diddy Made Millions Off Of 'Cheap Grapes'." Business Insider YouTube, March 13, 2018, www.youtube.com/watch?v=k2qgadSvNyU.

133 How Jay-Z And Diddy Made Millions Off Of 'Cheap Grapes'." Business Insider YouTube, March 13, 2018, www.youtube.com/watch?v=k2qgadSvNyU.

[134] "Hip-Hop's Future Billionaires." Forbes, www.forbes.com/pictures/eeel45edgm/hip-hops-future-billionaires-2.

[135] Millington, Alison. "How George Clooney and Two Friends Accidentally Created a 'Hangover-Free' Tequila Brand." Business Insider, June 22, 2017, uk.businessinsider.com/george-clooney-tequila-brand-casamigos-started-by-accident-2017-3.

[136] Felten, Eric. "Your 'Craft' Whiskey Is Probably From a Factory Distillery in Indiana." The Daily Beast, July 28, 2014, www.thedailybeast.com/your-craft-whiskey-is-probably-from-a-factory-distillery-in-indiana.

[137] "National Beer Sales & Production Data." Brewers Association, 2018, www.brewersassociation.org/statistics/national-beer-sales-production-data.

[138] "Report Finds More Than 1,280 Active Craft Spirits Producers in U.S." American Craft Spirits Association, May 9, 2016, americancraftspirits.org/report-finds-more-than-1280-active-craft-spirits-producers-in-u-s.

[139] "Craft Spirits Producers Sold Nearly 6 Million Cases Last Year Alone." American Craft Spirits Association, October 24, 2017, americancraftspirits.org/craft-spirits-producers-sold-nearly-6-million-cases-last-year-alone.

[140] "MADD Virgin Drinks Available Exclusively at 2,600 Walgreens Drugstores." PRNewswire, June 9, 2014, www.ireachcontent.com/news-releases/madd-virgin-drinks-available-exclusively-at-2600-walgreens-drugstores-262389041.html.

[141] "Topic: Restaurant Industry in the U.S - Statistics & Facts" Statista, www.statista.com/topics/1135/us-restaurants.

[142] "State of the Industry 2017." National Restaurant Association, 2017, www.restaurant.org/News-Research/Research/soi.

[143] "Top 100 Independents: The Ranking." Restaurant Business, 2017, www.restaurantbusinessonline.com/top-100-independents-2017/del-posto.

[144] Abend, Lisa. "The Cult of the Celebrity Chef Goes Global." Time, June 21, 2010, content.time.com/time/magazine/article/0,9171,1995844,00.html.

[145] "America's 25 Most Successful Chefs of 2017." The Daily Meal, 2017, www.thedailymeal.com/eat/america-s-25-most-successful-chefs-2017-slideshow.

[146] Weekly, Las Vegas. "50 Must-Eat Las Vegas Meals." LasVegasSun.com, April 16, 2012, lasvegassun.com/news/2012/apr/16/50-must-eat-las-vegas-meals.

[147] "Vegas Uncork'd | Schedule." Vegas Uncork'd, 2018, vegasuncorked.com/schedule.

[148] Curtas, John. "Eating Las Vegas." Eating Las Vegas, April 1, 2018, www.eatinglv.com.

[149] Diamond, Krista. "Five Giant Cocktails To Try This Weekend." Eater Vegas, April 13, 2018, vegas.eater.com/2018/4/13/17227472/best-giant-cocktails-shareable-las-vegas-restaurants.

[150] Park on Fremont, 2017, parkonfremont.com.

[151] Fiddlestix – Gold Spike, 2018, goldspike.com/fiddlestix.

[152] Buzz Pop Cocktails®, 2018, www.buzzpopcocktails.com.

153 Schultz., E.J. "Las Vegas Adds a Bespoke Beer Brand to Its 'What Happens Here' Campaign." Ad Age, April 11, 2016, adage.com/article/cmo-strategy/beer-brand-added-vegas-campaign/303474.

154 Richards, Sarah Elizabeth. "How to End Your Sugar Addiction." CNN, Sepember 30, 2015, www.cnn.com/2015/09/30/health/ending-sugar-addiction/index.html.

155 "Nevada Prostitution and Solicitation Laws - FindLaw.com." Findlaw, statelaws.findlaw.com/nevada-law/nevada-prostitution-and-solicitation-laws.html.

156 Lee, Joseph. "Las Vegas Returns to Sinful Roots." CNNMoney, May 28, 2004, money.cnn.com/2004/05/28/news/midcaps/las_vegas.

157 "Australia's Thunder From Down Under." Vegas.com - Las Vegas Hotels, Shows, Tours, Clubs & More, 2018, www.vegas.com/shows/adult/thunder-from-down-under-las-vegas.

158 Magic Mike Live, 2018, magicmikelivelasvegas.com.

159 Stephen, Nigel. "Nevada Legalizes Male Prostitution." WOL-AM 1450, December 14, 2009, woldcnews.com/38971/nevada-legalizes-male-prostitution.

160 Daly, Ian. "Exclusive: Meet America's First Legal Male Prostitute." GQ, January 25, 2010, www.gq.com/story/americas-first-legal-male-prostitute.

161 Center for Drug Evaluation and Research. "Prescription Drug Advertising - Background on Drug Advertising." U.S. Food and Drug Administration Home Page, June 19, 2015, www.fda.gov/Drugs/ResourcesForYou/Consumers/PrescriptionDrug Advertising/ucm071964.htm.

[162] Ventola, C. Lee. "Direct-to-Consumer Pharmaceutical Advertising." National Center for Biotechnology Information, October 2011, www.ncbi.nlm.nih.gov/pmc/articles.

[163] Ventola, C. Lee. "Direct-to-Consumer Pharmaceutical Advertising." National Center for Biotechnology Information, October 2011, www.ncbi.nlm.nih.gov/pmc/articles.

[164] Tigas, Mike, Ryann Grochowski Jones, Charles Ornstein, and Lena Groeger. "Dollars for Docs." ProPublica, June 28, 2018, projects.propublica.org/docdollars.

[165] Donohue, Julie. "A History of Drug Advertising: The Evolving Roles of Consumers and Consumer Protection." National Center for Biotechnology Information, December 2006, www.ncbi.nlm.nih.gov/pmc.

[166] Entis, Laura. "DTC Pharma Ad Spending Slipped 4.6% in 2017: Kantar." MM&M, March 12, 2018, www.mmm-online.com/commercial/dtc-pharma-ad-spending-slipped-46-in-2017-kantar/article/750421.

[167] "Marketing And Direct-To-Consumer Advertising (DTCA) Of Pharmaceuticals." National Conference of State Legislatures, July 1, 2015, http://www.ncsl.org/research/health/marketing-and-advertising-of-pharmaceuticals.aspx

[168] Donohue, Julie. "A History of Drug Advertising: The Evolving Roles of Consumers and Consumer Protection." National Center for Biotechnology Information, December 2006, www.ncbi.nlm.nih.gov/pmc.

[169] Tom, Kottler. "Marketers Discuss Catalysts for Use of Behavioral Science Techniques." MM&M, April 4, 2018, www.mmm-online.com/sponsored/marketers-discuss-catalysts-for-use-of-

behavioral-science-techniques/article/754156.

[170] Lazarus, David. "Direct-to-Consumer Drug Ads: A Bad Idea That's about to Get Worse." Los Angeles Times, February 15, 2017, www.latimes.com/business/la-fi-lazarus-drugadvertising-20170215-story.html.

[171] McCaffrey, Kevin. "How Pharma Marketers Are Using Behavioral Science." MM&M, April 5, 2017, www.mmm-online.com/commercial/pharma-healthcare-marketing-behavior-behavioral-science/article/648437.

[172] McCaffrey, Kevin. "How Pharma Marketers Are Using Behavioral Science." MM&M, April 5, 2017, www.mmm-online.com/commercial/pharma-healthcare-marketing-behavior-behavioral-science/article/648437.

[173] Primack, Brian A. MD, PhD; Mary V. Carroll, BA; Megan McNamara, MD, MSc; Mary Lou Klem, PhD, MLS; Brandy King, MLIS; Michael O. Rich, MD, MPH; Chun W. Chan, MD, MPH; Smita Nayak, MD. "Role of Video Games in Improving Health-Related Outcomes." National Center for Biotechnology Information, June 2012, https://www.ncbi.nlm.nih.gov/pmc/articles/PMC3391574/

[174] Baer, Stephen. "Game-Based Learning Helps Big Pharma Get Ahead." Forbes, May 11, 2017, www.forbes.com/sites/forbesagencycouncil/2017/05/11/game-based-learning-helps-big-pharma-get-ahead/2.

[175] Geiler, Kerry. "Protein Folding: The Good, the Bad, and the Ugly." Harvard University The Graduate School of Arts and Sciences, February 28, 2010, sitn.hms.harvard.edu/flash/2010/issue65.

[176] Coren, Michael J. "Foldit Gamers Solve Riddle of HIV Enzyme

within 3 Weeks." Scientific American, September 20, 2011, www.scientificamerican.com/article/foldit-gamers-solve-riddle.

[177] Baer, Stephen. "Game-Based Learning Helps Big Pharma Get Ahead." Forbes, May 11, 2017, www.forbes.com/sites/forbesagencycouncil/2017/05/11/game-based-learning-helps-big-pharma-get-ahead/2.

[178] "Suicide Claims More Lives than War, Murder, and Natural Disasters Combined." American Foundation for Suicide Prevention, 2015, afsp.donordrive.com/index.cfm.

[179] "Treating Depression – Psychotherapy or Medication?" American Psychiatric Association, April 17, 2017, www.psychiatry.org/newsroom/apa-blogs/apa-blog/2017/04/treating-depression-psychotherapy-or-medication.

[180] "What Is Depression?" American Psychiatric Association, January 2017, www.psychiatry.org/patients-families/depression/what-is-depression.

[181] Schulz, Kathryn. "Did Antidepressants Depress Japan?" The New York Times, August 22, 2004, www.nytimes.com/2004/08/22/magazine/did-antidepressants-depress-japan.html.

[182] Schulz, Kathryn. "Did Antidepressants Depress Japan?" The New York Times, August 22, 2004, www.nytimes.com/2004/08/22/magazine/did-antidepressants-depress-japan.html.

[183] Landers, Peter. "Drug Companies Push Japan To Change View of Depression." The Wall Street Journal, October 9, 2002, www.wsj.com/articles/SB1034112324618397796?ns=prod/accounts-wsj.

[184] Schulz, Kathryn. "Did Antidepressants Depress Japan?" The New York Times, August 22, 2004, www.nytimes.com/2004/08/22/magazine/did-antidepressants-depress-japan.html.

[185] Landers, Peter. "Drug Companies Push Japan To Change View of Depression." The Wall Street Journal, October 9, 2002, www.wsj.com/articles/SB1034112324618397796?ns=prod/accounts-wsj.

[186] Schulz, Kathryn. "Did Antidepressants Depress Japan?" The New York Times, August 22, 2004, www.nytimes.com/2004/08/22/magazine/did-antidepressants-depress-japan.html.

[187] Brady, Alison. "Film Explores Antidepressant Use in Japan." The Japan Times, July 12, 2007, www.japantimes.co.jp/news/2007/07/12/national/film-explores-antidepressant-use-in-japan.

[188] "Abilify Lawsuits." ConsumerSafety.org, 2018, www.consumersafety.org/legal/abilify-lawsuit.

[189] "$19.5 Million Settlement Reached in Deceptive Marketing of Abilify." Recall Report, January 2, 2017, www.recallreport.org/2017/01/19-5-million-settlement-reached-deceptive-marketing-abilify.

[190] Friedman, Richard A. "A Call for Caution on Antipsychotic Drugs." The New York Times, September 24, 2012, www.nytimes.com/2012/09/25/health/a-call-for-caution-in-the-use-of-antipsychotic-drugs.html?_r=0.

[191] Levine, Art. "Abilify Is Top-Selling U.S. Drug -- But New Reports Question Long-Term Antipsychotic Use, Cite Need for Personalized Services." The Huffington Post, December 12, 2014,

www.huffingtonpost.com/art-levine/abilify-is-top-selling-us_b_6282684.html.

[192] Friedman, Richard A. "A Call for Caution on Antipsychotic Drugs." The New York Times, September 24, 2012, www.nytimes.com/2012/09/25/health/a-call-for-caution-in-the-use-of-antipsychotic-drugs.html?_r=0.

[193] Friedman, Richard A. "A Call for Caution on Antipsychotic Drugs." The New York Times, September 24, 2012, www.nytimes.-com/2012/09/25/health/a-call-for-caution-in-the-use-of-antipsychotic-drugs.html?_r=0.

[194] Friedman, Richard A. "A Call for Caution on Antipsychotic Drugs." The New York Times, September 24, 2012, www.nytimes.com/2012/09/25/health/a-call-for-caution-in-the-use-of-antipsychotic-drugs.html?_r=0.

[195] Wolf, Z. Byron. "This Feels like a Tipping Point on Marijuana Legalization." CNN, June 28, 2018, www.cnn.com/2018/06/27/politics/marijuana-legalization-tipping-point/index.html.

[196] Marks, Gene. "HP Finds an Opportunity in the Marijuana Industry." The Washington Post, April 13, 2018, www.washingtonpost.com/news/on-small-business/wp/2018/04/13/hp-is-jumping-into-the-pot-business/?noredirect=on.

[197] Laslo, Matt. "Pot for All: How Congress Is Trying to Make Weed Legal." Rolling Stone, May 29, 2018, www.rollingstone.com/politics/politics-features/pot-for-all-how-congress-is-trying-to-make-weed-legal-628538.

[198] Lopez, German. "Marijuana Has Been Legalized in Nine States and Washington, DC." Vox, June 26, 2018,

www.vox.com/cards/marijuana-legalization/where-is-marijuana-legal.

[199] "Marijuana and Pain." Marijuana as Medicine?: the Science beyond the Controversy, by Alison Mack and Janet E. Joy, National Academy Press, 2001.

[200] Geiger, Abigail. "About Six-in-Ten Americans Support Marijuana Legalization." Pew Research Center, January 5, 2018, www.pewresearch.org/fact-tank/2018/01/05/americans-support-marijuana-legalization.

[201] Williams, Sean. "Is Marijuana the Answer to the Opioid Epidemic? Some Seniors Believe So." The Motley Fool, July 14, 2018, www.fool.com/investing/2018/07/14/is-marijuana-the-answer-to-the-opioid-epidemic-som.aspx.

[202] Delkic, Melina. "Legal Marijuana Is Supported by Every Group in America except Jeff Sessions, Republicans and Old People." Newsweek, January 11, 2018, www.newsweek.com/marijuana-supported-americans-except-sessions-republicans-778530.

[203] Roberts, Chris. "Sensing Big Bucks, Tobacco Companies Pivot Toward Marijuana." Observer, March 2, 2018, observer.com/2018/03/legalization-has-tobacco-companies-interested-in-marijuana-industry.

[204] Quinn, Greg. "Marijuana Will Become Legal in Canada on Oct. 17, Trudeau Says." Bloomberg.com, June 19, 2018, www.bloomberg.com/news/articles/2018-06-19/legal-pot-gets-green-light-after-canadian-senators-sign-off.

[205] Owram, Kristine. "Big money tests marijuana waters, with hedge funds leading charge." Bloomberg, July 13, 2018, https://www.msn.com/en-us/money/savingandinvesting/big-money-

tests-marijuana-waters-with-hedge-funds-leading-charge/ar-AAzXYuQ?li=BBnbfcN

[206] Canopy Growth Corporation, www.canopygrowth.com.

[207] "Leadership Team." Canopy Growth Corporation, https://www.canopygrowth.com/about/leadership-team.

[208] Owram, Kristine. "Big money tests marijuana waters, with hedge funds leading charge." Bloomberg, July 13, 2018, https://www.msn.com/en-us/money/savingandinvesting/big-money-tests-marijuana-waters-with-hedge-funds-leading-charge/ar-AAzXYuQ?li=BBnbfcN

[209] Quinn, Greg. "Marijuana Will Become Legal in Canada on Oct. 17, Trudeau Says." Bloomberg.com, June 19, 2018, www.bloomberg.com/news/articles/2018-06-19/legal-pot-gets-green-light-after-canadian-senators-sign-off.

[210] Schultz., E.J. "Cannabis Is Thriving but Brands like MedMen Still Find Buying Ads a Slow Burn." Ad Age, April 3, 2018, adage.com/article/cmo-strategy/cannabis-thriving-big-media-outlets-say-no-medmen/312965.

[211] Kohut, Tim. "LA Dispensary Launches The Largest Cannabis Marketing Campaign." High Times, January 5, 2018, hightimes.com/news/la-dispensary-launches-largest-cannabis-marketing-campaign.

[212] Kohut, Tim. "LA Dispensary Launches The Largest Cannabis Marketing Campaign." High Times, January 5, 2018, hightimes.com/news/la-dispensary-launches-largest-cannabis-marketing-campaign.

[213] Stanley, T.L. "With $2 Million Ad Push, Cannabis Retailer

MedMen Hopes to Finally Ditch the 'Stoner' Cliche." Adweek, April 6, 2018, www.adweek.com/creativity/with-2-million-ad-push-cannabis-retailer-madmen-hopes-to-finally-ditch-the-stoner-cliche.

[214] Schultz., E.J. "Cannabis Is Thriving but Brands like MedMen Still Find Buying Ads a Slow Burn." Ad Age, April 3, 2018, adage.com/article/cmo-strategy/cannabis-thriving-big-media-outlets-say-no-medmen/312965.

[215] Powell, Burgess. "The Countries With The Most Relaxed Weed Laws." High Times, February 28, 2018, hightimes.com/culture/countries-relaxed-weed-laws.

[216] "Dutch MPs Vote in Favour of Regulated Cannabis Cultivation." The Telegraph, February 21, 2017, www.telegraph.co.uk/news/2017/02/21/dutch-mps-vote-favour-regulated-cannabis-cultivation.

[217] Packham, Colin. "Australia to Permit Medicinal Cannabis Exports in Bid to Capture Lucrative Market" Reuters, January 3, 2018, www.reuters.com/article/us-australia-cannabis/australia-to-permit-medicinal-cannabis-exports-in-bid-to-capture-lucrative-market-idUSKBN1ET0D2.

[218] Bennett, Chris. "Marijuana Farming Is Now For US Agriculture." AgWeb, January 8, 2018, www.agweb.com/article/marijuana-farming-is-now-for-us-agriculture-naa-chris-bennett.

[219] Snell, Kelsey. "Suicide Is Rising Among American Farmers As They Struggle To Keep Afloat." NPR, May 16, 2018, www.npr.org/2018/05/16/611727777/suicide-is-rising-among-american-farmers-as-they-struggle-to-keep-afloat.

[220] "What Is CBD?" Project CBD, 2018, www.projectcbd.org/about/what-cbd.

221 Lhooq, Michelle. "The Best CBD Products for the Tasteful Non-Stoner." NYMag, April 20, 2018, nymag.com/strategist/article/best-cbd-products.html.

222 Carrier, Stacie. "5 Health Benefits of CBD Oils." Canabo Medical Clinic, December 16, 2017, www.canabomedicalclinic.com/5-health-benefits-cbd-oils.

223 Fraser, Carly. "Top 10 Best Plant-Based Natural Sunscreens." Live Love Fruit, May 21, 2013, livelovefruit.com/plant-based-natural-sunscreens.

224 Chamberlain, Craig. "Research Suggests Sexual Appeals in Ads Don't Sell Brands, Products." Illinois News Bureau, June 22, 2017, news.illinois.edu/view/6367/522402.

225 Castleman, Michael. "A New Study Reveals Our Deepest Sexual Insecurities." Psychology Today, May 14, 2016, www.psychologytoday.com/us/blog/all-about-sex/201605/new-study-reveals-our-deepest-sexual-insecurities.

226 Fenner, Justin. "Welcome to the Ball Sweat Economy." GQ, September 23, 2016, www.gq.com/story/ball-sweat-grooming-products.

227 Patel, Neel V. "You Are Disgusting in so Many Ways. Scientists Just Outlined Six of Them." Popular Science, June 5, 2018, www.popsci.com/evolution-disgust.

228 Spitznagel, Eric. "Now Deodorant Companies Are Eyeing Men's Balls." Tonic, June 6, 2017, tonic.vice.com/en_us/article/ev4d3z/now-deodorant-companies-are-eyeing-mens-balls.

229 Neff, Jack. "Is 'Fresh Balls' the Final Frontier in Male Grooming?"

Ad Age, June 6, 2012, adage.com/article/adages/fresh-balls-final-frontier-male-grooming/235191.

230 Spitznagel, Eric. "Now Deodorant Companies Are Eyeing Men's Balls." Tonic, June 6, 2017, tonic.vice.com/en_us/article/ev4d3z/now-deodorant-companies-are-eyeing-mens-balls.

231 Spitznagel, Eric. "Now Deodorant Companies Are Eyeing Men's Balls." Tonic, June 6, 2017, tonic.vice.com/en_us/article/ev4d3z/now-deodorant-companies-are-eyeing-mens-balls.

232 Hosie, Rachel. "More and More Men Are Buying Deodorant for Their Balls." The Independent, June 8, 2017, www.independent.co.uk/life-style/health-and-families/balls-deodorant-testicles-scrotum-hygiene-products-male-experts-ridiculous-a7778946.html.

233 Griffith, Erin. "Millennial Viagra Startup Hims Is Now Worth $200 Million." Wired, March 2, 2018, www.wired.com/story/millennial-viagra-startup-hims-is-now-worth-dollar200-million.

234 Conick, Hal. "Swipe Right: How Marketers Changed Online Dating." AMA, April 27, 2016, www.ama.org/publications/MarketingNews/Pages/swipe-right-how-marketers-changed-online-dating.aspx.

235 "The Way Strangers Meet via Dating Websites Is Changing Society in Unexpected Ways, Say Researchers." MIT Technology Review, October 10, 2017, www.technologyreview.com/s/609091/first-evidence-that-online-dating-is-changing-the-nature-of-society.

236 Marateck, Juliet. "Online Dating Lowers Self-Esteem, Increases Depression." CNN, May 29, 2018,

www.cnn.com/2018/05/29/health/online-dating-depression-study/index.html.

[237] "The Ugly Truth About Online Dating." Psychology Today, September 6, 2016, www.psychologytoday.com/us/blog/the-mating-game/201609/the-ugly-truth-about-online-dating.

[238] Paul, Aditi. "Cyberpsychology, Behavior, and Social Networking." Mary Ann Liebert Inc. Publishers, October 1, 2014, www.liebertpub.com/toc/cyber/17/10.

[239] Conick, Hal. "Swipe Right: How Marketers Changed Online Dating." AMA, April 27, 2016, www.ama.org/publications/MarketingNews/Pages/swipe-right-how-marketers-changed-online-dating.aspx.

[240] Smith, Aaron. "15% Of American Adults Have Used Online Dating Sites or Mobile Dating Apps." Pew Research Center, February 11, 2016, www.pewinternet.org/2016/02/11/15-percent-of-american-adults-have-used-online-dating-sites-or-mobile-dating-apps.

[241] "The Ugly Truth About Online Dating." Psychology Today, September 6, 2016, www.psychologytoday.com/us/blog/the-mating-game/201609/the-ugly-truth-about-online-dating.

[242] "Tinder's latest feature, Tinder U, is only for college students." TechCrunch, August 21, 2018, https://techcrunch.com/2018/08/21/tinders-latest-feature-tinder-u-is-only-for-college-students/.

[243] Conick, Hal. "Swipe Right: How Marketers Changed Online Dating." American Marketing Association, April 27, 2016, www.ama.org/publications/MarketingNews/Pages/swipe-right-how-marketers-changed-online-dating.aspx.

[244] Conick, Hal. "Swipe Right: How Marketers Changed Online Dating." American Marketing Association, 27 Apr. 2016, www.ama.org/publications/MarketingNews/Pages/swipe-right-how-marketers-changed-online-dating.aspx.

[245] Gerdau, Axel. "AI Sex Dolls Are Driving China's Sexual Revolution." VICE News, January 19, 2018, news.vice.com/en_us/article/yw54wj/ai-sex-dolls-are-driving-chinas-sexual-revolution.

[246] Gerdau, Axel. "AI Sex Dolls Are Driving China's Sexual Revolution." VICE News, January 19, 2018, news.vice.com/en_us/article/yw54wj/ai-sex-dolls-are-driving-chinas-sexual-revolution.

[247] "Meet Harmony The Sex Robot." VICELAND. March 14, 2018, https://www.youtube.com/watch?v=orBH_Qnw3eY

[248] Accomando, Beth, Katie Schoolov, Matthew Bowler, and Nicholas McVicker. "San Marcos-Based RealDoll Launches AI Sex Dolls." KPBS Public Media, April 20, 2018, www.kpbs.org/news/2018/apr/20/realdoll-launches-ai-sex-dolls.

[249] "There's a New Sex Robot in Town: Say Hello to Solana." Realdoll, 2018, www.engadget.com/2018/01/10/there-s-a-new-sex-robot-in-town-say-hello-to-solana.

[250] "Meet Harmony The Sex Robot." VICELAND. March 14, 2018, https://www.youtube.com/watch?v=orBH_Qnw3eY

[251] Trout, Christopher. "RealDoll's First Sex Robot Took Me to the Uncanny Valley." Engadget, April 11, 2011, www.engadget.com/2017/04/11/realdolls-first-sex-robot-took-me-to-the-uncanny-valley.

252 Griffith, Erin. "Henry the Sexbot Wants to Know All Your Hopes and Dreams." Wired, May 15, 2018, www.wired.com/story/henry-the-sexbot-wants-to-know-all-your-hopes-and-dreams.

253 Accomando, Beth, Katie Schoolov, Matthew Bowler, and Nicholas McVicker. "San Marcos-Based RealDoll Launches AI Sex Dolls." KPBS Public Media, April 20, 2018, www.kpbs.org/news/2018/apr/20/realdoll-launches-ai-sex-dolls.

254 Nevett, Joshua. "Las Vegas Strip Clubs 'to Replace Showgirls with SEX ROBOTS to Pull in Punters'." Dailystar.co.uk, January 20, 2018, www.dailystar.co.uk/news/latest-news/675423/las-vegas-strip-clubs-sex-robots-dolls-replace-showgirls-strippers-ces-sapphire.

255 Moye, David, and Chris McGonigal. "World's First Sex Doll Brothel Caters To Those Who Don't Want Human Touch." The Huffington Post, April 18, 2018, www.huffingtonpost.com/entry/worlds-first-sex-doll-brothel-caters-to-those-who-dont-want-human-touch_us_5ad76787e4b03c426daa9249.

256 Schäfer, Madlen. "Zu Besuch in Deutschlands Erstem Sexpuppen-Bordell." Vice, October 24, 2017, www.vice.com/de/article/a37g7k/zu-besuch-in-deutschlands-erstem-sexpuppen-bordell.

257 Schäfer, Madlen. "Zu Besuch in Deutschlands Erstem Sexpuppen-Bordell." Vice, October 24, 2017, www.vice.com/de/article/a37g7k/zu-besuch-in-deutschlands-erstem-sexpuppen-bordell.

258 Schäfer, Madlen. "Zu Besuch in Deutschlands Erstem Sexpuppen-Bordell." Vice, October 24, 2017, www.vice.com/de/article/a37g7k/zu-besuch-in-deutschlands-erstem-sexpuppen-bordell.

259 Moye, David, and Chris McGonigal. "World's First Sex Doll Brothel Caters To Those Who Don't Want Human Touch." The Huffington Post, April 18, 2018, www.huffingtonpost.com/entry/worlds-first-sex-doll-brothel-caters-to-those-who-dont-want-human-touch_us_5ad76787e4b03c426daa9249.

260 Constine, Josh. "Instagram Launches IGTV App for Creators, 1-Hour Video Uploads." TechCrunch, June 20, 2018, techcrunch.com/2018/06/20/igtv.

261 Papisova, Vera. "Everything You Need to Know About Pansexuality." Teen Vogue, April 27, 2018, www.teenvogue.com/story/what-is-pansexuality.

262 Castleman, Michael. "Great Sex Without Intercourse - Older Couples, Erectile Dysfunction." AARP, www.aarp.org/home-family/sex-intimacy/info-12-2012/great-sex-without-intercourse.html.

263 Sorrel, Charlie. "A German Politician Proposes A Program For Sex Workers To Service Senior Citizens." Fast Company, January 18, 2017, www.fastcompany.com/3067085/a-german-politician-proposes-a-program-for-sex-workers-to-service-senior-citizens.

264 "Sexualassistenz: Grüne Fordern Sex Auf Rezept Für Pflegebedürftige." ZEIT ONLINE, January 8, 2017, www.zeit.de/politik/deutschland/2017-01/sexualassistenz-gruene-sex-schwerkranke.

265 O'Kane, Caitlin. "Sonic Blends Beef and Mushrooms for More Eco-Friendly Burger." CBS News, March 7, 2018, www.cbsnews.com/news/sonic-blends-beef-and-mushrooms-for-more-eco-friendly-burger.

266 Gaulhiac, Nathalie. "A Tiny German Startup That Makes Protein Beer Is Taking off after Winning the Country's Largest Fitness Fair."

Business Insider, May 25, 2018, www.businessinsider.com/germans-tristan-bruemmer-and-erik-dimter-develop-protein-beer-called-joybraeu-2018-5.

[267] McMillan, Tracie. "Menu of the Future: Insects, Weeds, and Bleeding Veggie Burgers." National Geographic, March 8, 2018, www.nationalgeographic.com/environment/future-of-food/future-of-food-agriculture-ecology.

[268] Gerdau, Axel. "AI Sex Dolls Are Driving China's Sexual Revolution." VICE News, January 19, 2018, news.vice.com/en_us/article/yw54wj/ai-sex-dolls-are-driving-chinas-sexual-revolution.

[269] "Artificial Intelligence Already Revolutionizing Pharma." PharmExec.com, January 10, 2018, www.pharmexec.com/artificial-intelligence-already-revolutionizing-pharma.

[270] "Sex, lies and A.I. – How Americans feel about Artificial Intelligence," SYZYGY, October 2017, https://think.syzygy.net/ai-report/us#download

[271] "Sex, lies and A.I. – How Americans feel about Artificial Intelligence," SYZYGY, October 2017, https://think.syzygy.net/ai-report/us#download

[272] Solon, Olivia. "More than 70% of US Fears Robots Taking over Our Lives, Survey Finds." The Guardian, October 4, 2017, www.theguardian.com/technology/2017/oct/04/robots-artificial-intelligence-machines-us-survey.

[273] Gelb, Paul. "Branding, Marketing, and the Impact of Self-Driving Cars." AMA, November 30, 2017, www.ama.org/publications/eNewsletters/Marketing-News-Weekly/Pages/marketing-impact-self-driving-cars.aspx.

[274] Reinhart, RJ. "Americans Upbeat on Artificial Intelligence, but Still Wary." Gallup.com, January 31, 2018, news.gallup.com/poll/226502/americans-upbeat-artificial-intelligence-wary.aspx.

[275] O'Reilly, Lara. "A Japanese Ad Agency Invented an AI Creative Director - and Ad Execs Preferred Its Ad to a Human's." Business Insider, Business Insider, March 12, 2017, www.businessinsider.com/mccann-japans-ai-creative-director-creates-better-ads-than-a-human-2017-3.

[276] Stephen, Andrew. "AI Is Changing Marketing As We Know It, And That's A Good Thing." Forbes, October 31, 2017, www.forbes.com/sites/andrewstephen/2017/10/30/ai-is-changing-marketing-as-we-know-it-and-thats-a-good-thing.

[277] "Neil Davidson of HeyHuman: How Brands Can Humanise AI." More About Advertising, October 4, 2017, www.moreaboutadvertising.com/2017/10/neil-davidson-of-heyhuman-how-brands-can-help-humanise-ai.

[278] Bergland, Christopher. "This Is Your Brain Binging on Food, Sex, Alcohol, or Drugs." Psychology Today, May 31, 2016, www.psychologytoday.com/us/blog/the-athletes-way/201605/is-your-brain-binging-food-sex-alcohol-or-drugs.

[279] Marsch, Lisa A., and Jacob T. Borodovsky. "Technology-Based Interventions for Preventing and Treating Substance Use Among Youth." National Center for Biotechnology Information, August 3, 2016, www.ncbi.nlm.nih.gov/pmc.

[280] ElTayeby O., Eaglin T., Abdullah M., Burlinson D., Dou W., Yao L. (2017) Detecting Drinking-Related Contents on Social Media by Classifying Heterogeneous Data Types. In: Benferhat S., Tabia K., Ali M. (eds) Advances in Artificial Intelligence: From Theory to Practice.

IEA/AIE 2017. Lecture Notes in Computer Science, vol 10351. Springer, Cham.

[281] Livernois, Cara. "Researchers Develop Machine Learning App That Predicts Overeating Tendencies." Clinical Innovation + Technology, December 15, 2017, www.clinical-innovation.com/topics/artificial-intelligence/researchers-develop-machine-learning-app-predicts-overeating.

ACKNOWLEDGMENTS

Thanks to Traci Mann, Ph.D., for her candor and passion about food and eating. It was thrilling to hear a prominent scientist swear during an interview.

Thanks to Andy McClellan for his insight, wit, and deep knowledge of the alcohol industry. Now I know I should roll my eyes at anyone who demands Tito's Vodka at a sports bar.

Thanks to Chris Conrad for his comprehensive, thoughtful responses to my questions about the current state and future of cannabis in the United States. You opened my mind to possibilities I hadn't imagined.

Thanks to Laura Rademacher, MA, LMFT, CST, for offering judgment-free insight into human sexual needs. You reminded me that everyone deserves pleasure.

ABOUT THE AUTHOR

Founder of THINC B2B Digital Marketing and Management Consultants, Tony Harris is close to the brands that define the parameters of our digital lifestyles. He travels extensively providing counsel to clients around the globe, and in his spare time collects travel stories to share with friends and family, alongside a good cigar.

www.thefadsbook.com

 facebook.com/thefadsbook

 twitter.com/thefadsbook

 instagram.com/thefadsbook

38805153R00104

Made in the USA
San Bernardino, CA
14 June 2019